*Readings in Literary Criticism 11*
# CRITICS ON MATTHEW ARNOLD

*Readings in Literary Criticism*

(*Nos. 12–15 are in preparation*)

# CRITICS ON MATTHEW ARNOLD

*Readings in Literary Criticism*

Edited by Jacqueline E. M. Latham

London · George Allen and Unwin Ltd

FIRST PUBLISHED IN 1973

© *George Allen & Unwin Ltd* 1973

ISBN 0 04 821029 3

PRINTED IN GREAT BRITAIN
*in* 10 *point Plantin type*
BY CLARKE, DOBLE & BRENDON LTD
PLYMOUTH

# CONTENTS

# INTRODUCTION

In 1869 Matthew Arnold wrote in a letter to his mother, 'My poems represent, on the whole, the main movement of mind of the last quarter of a century, and thus they will probably have their day as people become conscious to themselves of what that movement of mind is, and interested in the literary productions which reflect it. It might be fairly urged that I have less poetical sentiment than Tennyson, and less intellectual vigour and abundance than Browning; yet, because I have perhaps more of a fusion of the two than either of them, and have more regularly applied that fusion to the main line of modern development, I am likely enough to have my turn, as they have had theirs.'

Arnold was right; his place as poet in the Victorian triumvirate is assured. But his eminence is no less secure on other grounds: as critic, thinker and prophet. These other roles are, perhaps, what Arnold had in mind when he so diffidently expressed his claim for poetic distinction, and there is no doubt that it is partly his intellectual stature which accounts for his importance and interest to us as a poet. Indeed, of the many books on Arnold published in the last two decades, most, including those primarily concerned with his poetry, have tracked his 'movement of mind' in relation to that of the age. The fact is that Arnold, perhaps more than any other man, sums up for us what seems best and most typical of the Victorian age. As a reforming school inspector he anticipates one of the central concerns of our own times and, bearing in mind the conditions of mid-nineteenth-century industrial England, he can also be seen as a man of heroic action. Furthermore, Arnold's scepticism in matters of religious dogma was allied to a strong moral and religious sense which reassures us that traditional values can be maintained when supernatural sanctions are withdrawn. Most important of all, Arnold's vain attempt to integrate his emotional and intellectual life provides an extreme case of that fragmentation suffered by so many of the great Victorians. Many of these aspects of Arnold's life are reflected in the essays and extracts from books brought together in this volume. However, it is with Arnold the poet that most of these critics are primarily concerned.

Mallarmé, writing to a friend, stressed that poems are made with words and not with ideas, and interesting though all Arnold's writings may be to us as a record of an exceptionally sensitive Victorian intelligence, his final status as a poet must depend upon his handling of words. I have therefore grouped together, near the beginning of this volume, extracts from a number of critics who specifically question the adequacy of Arnold's diction. Unfortunately no one has given a direct and convincing answer to this criticism, although as Professor Christopher Ricks rightly says, 'Verbal achievement is an essential issue whenever a poem is quoted.' The reader must, therefore, make up his own mind. In the case of 'Dover Beach' or 'To Marguerite—Continued' Arnold's success may seem clear, but one must consider carefully whether in 'Thyrsis' he is merely using a Romantic tradition, derived from Keats, which has become inadequate for what has to be said. Does the prosaic and flat style of part of 'Empedocles on Etna', Arnold's most ambitious poem, really serve the purposes of art, and is it enough, as W. E. Houghton suggests, that 'the form is at least equal, often more than equal, to the demands of a complex content'? How far is Arnold's poetry vitiated by the habit, which he deplored, of 'using poetry as a channel for thinking aloud instead of making anything'? Conversely, is he more successful as a poet when, observing the theories expressed in his Preface to the 1853 *Poems*, he strives for objectivity and *Architectonicè* and turns to a subject drawn from the remote past?

However, whatever the final status of Arnold as poet he must always retain his claim on us as a prophet and a man. It is a great loss that he asked that no biography should be written. Few have combined so profitably the active and the scholarly life, fighting clearsightedly for values which we in the second half of the twentieth century need quite as much as the Victorians did.

*Kingston Polytechnic*  
*Kingston-upon-Thames*

*J. E. M. Latham*

## ACKNOWLEDGEMENTS

We are grateful to the following for permission to use copyright material from the works whose titles follow in brackets:

The Johns Hopkins Press (A. H. Roper's *Arnold's Poetic Landscapes*); Harvard University Press (J. Hillis Miller's *The Disappearance of God*); The Clarendon Press, Oxford (F. W. Bateson's *English Poetry and English Language*); Yale University Press (George H. Ford's *Keats and the Victorians*); Methuen and Co. Ltd (R. A. Foakes' *The Romantic Assertion*); Victorian Studies, Indiana University (C. Ricks reviewing books on Arnold); Columbia University Press (Lionel Trilling's *Matthew Arnold*); Yale University Press (A. Dwight Culler's *Imaginative Reason*, © 1966 by Yale University); The Longman Group Ltd (J. D. Jump's *Matthew Arnold*); Murray Krieger ('Dover Beach' *and the Tragic Sense of Eternal Recurrence*); H. W. Fulweiler (*Matthew Arnold: the Metamorphosis of a Merman*, from *Victorian Poetry*); Macmillan (A. E. Dyson's *The Last Enchantments*, originally printed in *The Review of English Studies*, and recently published in *Between Two Worlds*); The University of Durham (Paul Edwards' *Hebraism, Hellenism, and* 'The Scholar-Gypsy'); Duke University Press (P. F. Baum's *Ten Studies in the Poetry of Matthew Arnold*); University of Toronto Press (Harvey Kerpneck's *The Road to Rugby Chapel*, reprinted from the *University of Toronto Quarterly*, Volume 34, January 1965 by permission of the author and the University of Toronto Press); Victorian Studies (W. E. Houghton's *Arnold's* 'Empedocles on Etna'); George Watson (*The Literary Critics*, published by Chatto and Windus).

We have been unable to trace the copyright holder of W. H. Mallock's *Every Man his Own Poet* and would welcome any information enabling us to do so.

# Some Nineteenth-Century Views

## W. M. ROSSETTI
### Arnold's Self-consciousness

If any one quality may be considered common to all living poets, it is that which we have heard aptly described as *self-consciousness*. In this many appear to see the only permanent trace of the now old usurping deluge of Byronism; but it is truly a fact of the time,—less a characteristic than a portion of it. Every species of composition—the dramatic, the narrative, the lyric, the didactic, the descriptive—is imbued with this spirit; and the reader may calculate with almost equal certainty on becoming acquainted with the belief of a poet as of a theologian or a moralist. Of the evils resulting from the practice, the most annoying and the worst is that some of the lesser poets, and all mere pretenders, in their desire to emulate the really great, feel themselves under a kind of obligation to assume opinions, vague, incongruous or exaggerated, often not only not their own, but the direct reverse of their own—a kind of meanness that has replaced, and goes far to compensate for, the flatteries of our literary ancestors. On the other hand, this quality has created a new tie of interest between the author and his public, enhances the significance of great works, and confers value on even the slightest productions of a true poet.

That the systematic infusion of this spirit into the drama and epic compositions is incompatible with strict notions of art will scarcely be disputed: but such a general objection does not apply in the case of lyric poetry, where even the character of the subject is optional. It is an instance of this kind that we are now about to consider. . . .

From the opening of a review of Arnold's first volume of poems, *The Strayed Reveller, and Other Poems,* in *The Germ,* 1850, pp. 84–96 (84). (The page numbers before the bracket give the beginning and end of the whole article; those within the bracket the pages of the actual extract.)

## J. A. FROUDE
### Poetic Discipline

. . . Whatever be the merits of the 'Strayed Reveller' as poetry, it is certainly not a poem in the sense which English people generally attach to the word, looking as they do not only for imaginative composition but for verse;—and as certainly if the following passage had been printed merely as prose, in a book which professed to be nothing else, no one would have suspected that it was composed of an agglutination of lines.

The gods are happy; they turn on all sides their shining eyes, and see below them earth and men. They see Tiresias sitting staff in hand on the warm grassy Asopus bank, his robe drawn over his old, sightless head, revolving inly the doom of Thebes. They see the Centaurs in the upper glens of Pelion, on the streams where the red-berried ashes fringe the clear brown shallow pools; with streaming flanks and heads reared proudly, snuffing the mountain wind. They see the Scythian on the wide steppe, unharnessing his wheeled house at noon; he tethers his beast down and makes his meal, mare's milk and bread baked on the embers; all around the boundless waving grass plains stretch, thick starred with saffron and the yellow hollyhock and flag-leaved iris flowers.

No one will deny that this is fine imaginative painting, and as such poetical,—but it is the poetry of well written, elegant prose. Instead of the recurring sounds, whether of rhyme or similarly weighted syllables, which constitute the outward form of what we call verse, we have the careless grace of uneven, undulating sentences, flowing on with a rhythmic cadence indeed, but free from all constraint of metre or exactitude of form. It may be difficult, perhaps it is impossible, to fix the measure of licence which a poet may allow himself in such matters, but it is at least certain that the greatest poets are those who have allowed themselves the fewest of such liberties: in art as in morals, and as in everything which man undertakes, true greatness is the most ready to recognize and most willing to obey those simple outward laws which have been sanctioned by the experience of mankind, and we suspect the originality which cannot move except on novel paths.

This is but one of several reasons which explain the apathy of the public on A.'s first appearance. There was large promise, but the public require performance; and in poetry a single failure overweighs a hundred successes. It was possible that his mistakes were the mistakes of a man whose face was in the right direction—who was feeling his way, and who would ultimately find it; but only time could decide if this were so; and in the interval, the coldness of his reception would serve to test the nature of his faculty.

So far we have spoken with reserve, for we have simply stated the feelings with which we regarded this little volume on first reading it; but the reserve is no longer necessary, and the misgivings which we experienced have not been justified. At the close of last year another volume was published, again of miscellaneous poems, which went beyond the most sanguine hopes of A.'s warmest admirers. As before with 'The Strayed Revellers', so again with 'Empedocles on Etna', the *pièce de résistance* was not the happiest selection. But of the remaining pieces, and of all those which he has more recently added, it is difficult to speak in too warm praise. In the unknown A., we are now to recognize a son of the late Master of Rugby, Dr Arnold. Like a good knight, we suppose he thought it better to win his spurs before appearing in public with so honoured a name; but the associations which belong to it will suffer no alloy from him who now wears it. Not only is the advance in art remarkable, in greater clearness of effect, and in the mechanical handling of words, but far more in simplicity and healthfulness of moral feeling. There is no more obscurity, and no mysticism; and we see everywhere the working of a mind bent earnestly on cultivating whatever is highest and worthiest in itself; of a person who is endeavouring, without affectation, to follow the best things, to see clearly what is good, and right, and true, and to fasten his heart upon these. There is usually a period in the growth of poets in which, like coarser people, they mistake the voluptuous for the beautiful; but in Mr Arnold there is no trace of any such tendency; pure, without effort, he feels no enjoyment and sees no beauty in the atmosphere of the common passions; and in nobleness of purpose, in a certain loftiness of mind singularly tempered with modesty, he continually reminds us of his father. There is an absence, perhaps, of colour; it is natural that it should be so in the earlier poems of a writer who proposes aims such as these to himself; his poetry is addressed to the intellectual, and not to the animal emotions; and to persons of animal taste, the flavour will no doubt be over simple; but it is true poetry—a true representation of true human feeling. It may not be immediately popular, but it will win its way in the long run, and has elements of endurance in it which enable it to wait without anxiety for recognition. . . .

From a review of Arnold's first three volumes of poetry in *The Westminster Review*, Vol. 61, 1854, pp. 146–59 (148–50).

## W. C. ROSCOE

### Damning with Faint Praise

. . . One of the few observations worth noting (if it be worth noting) in that strangely barren work, the *Life and Letters of Byron* is one in which his Lordship maintains that there are qualities in poetry closely corresponding with those which distinguish the gentleman in life, and that the same sort of vulgarity may be found in the false assumptions of art as in those of the world. Now Mr Arnold's are eminently the poems of a gentleman, and what is, perhaps, part of this characteristic, they are thoroughly genuine and sincere, the author is always himself and not a pretence at any one else; there is no affectation, no strained effort, no borrowed plumage; he presents himself without disguise, and without false shame; is dignified, simple, and self-restrained. If not always profound, at least he does not affect profundity; his strokes bring his thought or sentiment out clear and decisive; he is never guilty of false show and glitter, and those who have read some of our modern poets, will recognize the inestimable comfort of not having to press through an umbrageous forest of verbiage and heterogeneous metaphors in order to get at a thin thought concealed in its centre. There is artistic finish too in his verse (though, as we wish hereafter to remark, not in his conceptions); not the finish of high polish, but the refined ease and grace of a taste pure by nature and yet conscientiously cultivated. Hence instead of congratulating ourselves that we have read him, we find a pleasure in actually reading him, and take him up again and again with undiminished freshness and enjoyment. Partly it is that he does not make too great a demand upon us; his light free air refreshes us. Instead of being hemmed in by that majesty and terror which make the vicinity of the Alps oppressive, we stroll with lighter hearts on breezy heaths and uplands. Like Wordsworth, Mr Arnold owes part of his charm to the very absence of deep and engrossing feelings in his nature. . . .

From a review of Arnold's first three volumes of poetry in *The Prospective Review*, Vol. 10, 1854, pp. 99–118 (100–1).

## W. H. MALLOCK
### A Recipe

Take one soulfull of involuntary unbelief, which has been previously well flavoured with self-satisfied despair. Add to this one beautiful text of Scripture. Mix these well together; and as soon as ebullition commences grate in finely a few regretful allusions to the New Testament and the lake of Tiberias, one constellation of stars, half-a-dozen allusions to the nineteenth century, one to Goethe, one to Mont Blanc, or the Lake of Geneva; and one also, if possible, to some personal bereavement. Flavour the whole with a mouthful of 'faiths' and 'infinites' and a mixed mouthful of 'passions', 'finites', and 'yearnings'. This class of poem is concluded usually with some question about which we have to observe only that it shall be impossible to answer.

From *Every Man his Own Poet or the Inspired Singer's Recipe Book*, Thos Shrimpton and Son, Oxford, 1872, pp. 11–12.

## R. H. HUTTON
### Matthew Arnold's Themes

. . . Thus in all his poetical success, it is easy to distinguish two distinct strands: first, the clear recognition (with Goethe) of our spiritual unrest, and the manful effort to control it; next, the clear recognition (with Wordsworth) of the balm to be found in sincere communion with Nature. To the treatment of both these elements again he has given a certain freshness and individuality of his own.

We will first indicate generally his treatment of the former point. His characteristic effort on this side has been to introduce into a delineation, at once consistent and various in its aspects, of the intellectual difficulties, hesitations, and distresses of cultivated minds in the nineteenth century, a vein of imperious serenity—what he himself calls 'sanity' of treatment—which may stimulate the mind to bear the pain of constantly disappointed hope. Yet, oddly enough, his early theory of poetry would have restrained him from giving us such a picture of moral and intellectual sufferings at all; and he even suppressed a poem, 'Empedocles on Etna', which had already gained a certain reputation, and which, beneath a thin disguise of antiquity, discussed half the religious difficulties of modern days, simply because he declared it poetically faulty to choose a situation in which 'everything is to be endured, nothing to be done'. It was a condemnation of every successful poem he has written, emphatically so of the long expositions of our modern spiritual paralysis and fever in the two poems to the author of 'Obermann', of the lines at Heine's grave, of the stanzas at the Grand Chartreuse; indeed, we may say, of all his poems except the classic play *Merope*, which probably Mr Arnold himself now regards as a partial failure, since though now restored, he kept it back for a long time from his complete editions. 'Empedocles on Etna', according to Mr Arnold in his preface to the edition of 1853, was poetically faulty because it was a picture of 'a continuous state of mental distress, unrelieved by incident or hope', which is quite true, and not less true of almost all his other poems. But when he said that it was also unrelieved by *resistance*, he was unjust to himself. What alone renders all this delineation of moral distress and spiritual bewilderment which pervades this poem endurable is that there is a steady current of resistance, a uniform 'sanity' of self-control in the treatment of the painful symptoms so subtly described. Empedocles, in the course of his meditations on suicide on the slopes of Etna, no doubt dwells much on the feeble and false religious philosophy of the time, the credulous self-flatteries of human sophistry, and the sharp antagonism between clear self-knowledge and the superstitions of the age; but he also makes a vigorous appeal to the manliness, fortitude, and sobriety of spirit with which all the disappointments and failures of humanity ought to be met, asserts that it is the part of a man of true wisdom to curb immoderate desires, to bow to the might of forces he cannot control, and, while nursing no 'extravagant hope', to yield to no despair. And when, after thus completely justifying his own 'sanity of soul', he confesses himself unable to act as he approves and leaps into the fiery crater, the reader feels that the blunder of the poet has not been in painting the suffering too highly—for it is not highly coloured—but in selecting for the sufferer a man of too low a courage, and in making his acts a foil to his thoughts. So far from there being no resistance, no breakwater opposed to the flowing tides of mental suffering, Empedocles creates the sole interest of the poem by his manly swimming against the stream of despondency, to which later he suddenly abandons himself without sufficient cause assigned. It is like the story of the man who said 'I go not', and then went, without giving any glimpse of the reason for his change of mind—a story which, without any attempt to fill in the missing link, would certainly not be a sufficient subject for a poem. It seems to me striking enough that the very charm of Mr Arnold's method in dealing with this hectic fever of the modern intellect,—for Empedocles, if a true ancient, is certainly a still truer modern in his argument,—is due to his own inconsistency; is due, that is, to the fact that when his subject required him to paint and justify the last stages of moral despondency—and his intellectual view was sceptical enough to be in sympathy with his subject—he could not help expending his chief strength in cutting away the moral ground from under his hero's feet, by insisting that the well-spring of despair was, after all, not in the hostility of Nature or of human circumstances, but in the licence of immoderate desires and of insatiable self-will. And it is so throughout his poems. He cannot paint the restlessness of the soul— though he paints it vividly and well—without painting also the attitude of resistance to it, without giving the impression of a head held high above it, a nature that fixes the limits beyond which the corrosion of distrust and doubt shall not go, a deep speculative melancholy kept at bay, *not* by faith, but by a kind of domineering temperance of nature. This is the refrain of almost all his poems. He yields much to this melancholy—intellectually, we should say, almost everything—but morally, he bids it keep its distance, and forbids it to engulf him.

It is this singular equipoise between the doubts that devour, and the intrepid sobriety that excites him to resistance, which gives the peculiar tone to Mr Arnold's poems. He has not the impulse or *abandon* of nature for a pure lyric melancholy, such as Shelley could pour forth in words that almost make the heart weep, as, for instance, in the 'Lines Written in Dejection in Naples'. Again, Mr Arnold has nothing of the proud faith that conquers melancholy and that gives to the poems of Wordsworth their tone of rapture. Yet he hits a wonderful middle note between the two. The 'lyrical cry', as he himself has finely designated the voice in which the true poetic exaltation of feeling expresses itself, is to be found in a multitude of places in his poems; but in him it neither utters the dejection of the wounded spirit nor the joy of the victorious spirit, but rather the calm of a steadfast equanimity in conflict with an unconquerable and yet also unconquering destiny—a firm mind without either deep shadows of despair or high lights of faith, only the lucid dusk of an intellectual twilight. . . .

When I come to ask what Mr Arnold's poetry has done for this generation, the answer must be that no one has expressed more power-fully and poetically its spiritual weaknesses, its craving for a passion that it cannot feel, its admiration for a self-mastery that it cannot achieve, its desire for a creed that it fails to accept, its sympathy with a faith that it will not share, its aspiration for a peace that it does not know. But Mr Arnold does all this from the intellectual side,—sincerely and delicately, but from the surface, and never from the centre. It is the same with his criticisms. They are fine, they are keen, they are often true, but they are always too much limited to the thin superficial layer of the moral nature of their subjects, and seem to take little comparative interest in the deeper individuality beneath. Read his essay on Heine, and you will see the critic engrossed with the relation of Heine to the political and social ideas of his day, and passing over with comparative indifference the true soul of Heine, the fountain both of his poetry and his cynicism. Read his fine lectures on translating Homer, and observe how exclusively the critic's mind is occupied with the form, as distinguished from the substance of the Homeric poetry. Even when he concerns himself with the greatest modern poets, with Shakespeare (as in the preface to the earlier edition of his poems), or with Goethe in reiterated poetical criticisms, or when he, again and again in his poems, treats of Wordsworth, it is always the style and superficial doctrine of their poetry, not the individual character and unique genius which occupy him. He will tell you whether a poet is 'sane and clear', or stormy and fervent; whether he is 'rapid' and 'noble', or loquacious and quaint; whether a thinker penetrates the husks of conventional thought which mislead the crowd; whether there is sweetness as well as lucidity in his aims; whether a descriptive writer has 'distinction' of style, or is admirable only for his vivacity; but he rarely goes to the individual heart of any of the subjects of his criticism;—he finds their style and class, but not their personality in that class; he *ranks* his men, but does not portray them; hardly even seems to find much interest in the *individual* roots of their character. And so, too, with his main poetical theme,—the spiritual weakness and languor and self disdain of the age. He paints these characteristics in language which makes his poems a sort of natural voice for the experience of his contemporaries, a voice without which their intellectual life would be even more obscure and confused than it is; but still with a certain intellectual superficiality of touch which suggests the sympathetic observer rather than the wakeful sufferer, and which leaves an unfathomed depth beneath the layer of perturbed consciousness with which he deals—that is, beneath that plane wherein the spheres of the intellect and the soul intersect, of which he has so carefully studied the currents and the tides. The sign of this limitation, of this exclusion, of this externality of touch, is the tinge of conscious intellectual majesty rearing its head above the storm with the 'Quos ego' of Virgil's god, that never forsakes these poems of Mr Arnold's even when their 'lyrical cry' is most pathetic. It is this which identifies him with the sceptics, which renders his poems, pathetic as they often are, no adequate expression of the passionate craving of the soul for faith. There is always a tincture of pride in his confessed inability to believe—a self-congratulation that he is too clear-eyed to yield to the temptations of the heart. He asks with compassionate imperiousness for demonstration rather than conviction; conviction he will not take without demonstration. The true *humility* of the yearning for faith is far from Mr Arnold's conception.

From *Literary Essays*, 3rd edition, Macmillan and Co., London, 1888, pp. 317–20 and 350–2.

# Modern Critics on Matthew Arnold

# Arnold and Nature - Two Views

## A. ROPER

### The Victorian Dilemma

. . . Although my primary object is a critical description of some ways in which landscape poetry has been written, I have found that analysis of Thomson, Gray, and Collins provides terms more immediately appropriate to Arnold than could be derived from a similar analysis of the Romantic poets. The reason is no doubt partly historical: very generally, the Augustans and Victorians share a strongly objective sense of nature and landscape as something to be reflected upon, examined for evidence of transcendent truth, or used as the correlative of a mood. What, in general, they do not share is a Romantic conviction that behind the objective phenomena known to the senses there are truths or realities apprehensible by an exercise of the imagination which eliminates the distinction between subjective observer and observed object. In some ways, it is true, the Victorians were unlucky inheritors of disparate elements from the Augustan and Romantic traditions. They share the Augustan separateness of subject and object, but are not sustained by the Augustan habit of finding in nature a system of social relationships relevant to the social preoccupations of man. The habit is denied them because they share the Romantic belief that the 'truths' of nature are relevant for the individual observer as individual, not as representative member of society. Arnold, especially, scans nature with Augustan eyes in search of something like Romantic 'truths', but having lost the secret of the Romantic way of finding them.[1] The characteristic melancholy of this poetry marks the unavoidable failure of such an endeavour. The result of this disparate inheritance was the familiar picture of Victorian man alone in an alien universe, unable to follow the Augustan in finding lessons in nature for the social and urban life of man and equally unable to follow the Romantics in asserting or assuming the social life of man to be irrelevant to the lessons of nature, except when nature taught that society should respect individual dignity. The major

[1] This 'Victorian' disjunction is phrased somewhat differently by Herbert R. Coursen, Jr, ' "The Moon Lies Fair": The Poetry of Matthew Arnold', *Studies in English Literature*, Vol. 4, 1964, pp. 569–81: 'In that he can be placed "between two traditions", Arnold might be called the representative Victorian poet; he is Romantic in his use of the symbolic landscape, Modern in his finding there only negation' (p. 581).

poetic document of this simultaneous desire and failure to unite nature and human society is, of course, 'Empedocles on Etna'. . . .

From *Arnold's Poetic Landscapes*, Johns Hopkins Press, Baltimore, 1969, pp. 8–9.

# J. HILLIS MILLER

## Spiritual Failure

. . . Arnold has no sense of a harmonizing power in nature, nor can he express the Coleridgean sense that each object, though unique, is at the same time a symbol of the totality. Each object means itself, and is not a symbol of anything further. Landscapes in his poetry are often a neutral backdrop before which the action takes place. The closest Arnold can come to the multi-dimensional symbolism of romantic poetry is the simple equation of allegory, in which some human meaning or value is attached from the outside to a natural object. This produces locutions in which a concrete thing and an abstraction are yoked by violence together, as in the 'sea of life', the 'Sea of Faith', the 'vasty hall of death', the 'icebergs of the past', and so on. Try as he will Arnold cannot often get depth and resonance in his landscapes, and his descriptive passages tend to become unorganized lists of natural objects. The disorder and flatness of these lists betray Arnold's sense that nature is just a collection of discrete things, all jumbled up together, with no pattern or hierarchy. Arnold's nature, like his own life, is repetitive, the repetition of more examples of the same objects, or of more views of the same disorder. In 'Resignation', he describes his return with his sister to a scene he has visited ten years before. 'Here sit we', he says, 'and again unroll,/ Though slowly, the familiar whole.' The scene is not really, it turns out, a 'whole'. There is no transfiguration of a revisited scene, as in 'Tintern Abbey', and the suggestions of continuity in 'unroll' are not supported by what follows:

> The solemn wastes of heathy hill
> Sleep in the July sunshine still;
> The self-same shadows now, as then,
> Play through this grassy upland glen;
> The loose dark stones on the green way
> Lie strewn, it seems, where then they lay;
> On this mild bank above the stream,
> (You crush them!) the blue gentians gleam.
> Still this wild brook, the rushes cool,
> The sailing foam  the shining pool!

Hill, shadows, gentians; brook, rushes, foam  pool—the scene is a collection of the elements which happen by accident to be there, 'strewn' about like the haphazard stones which lie in the centre of the picture.

There is no grouping, no inner force moulding all to a unity, no 'instress' such as Hopkins finds in nature, no interior tendency toward pattern or form. Everything is slack. The scene, if it expresses anything, expresses the disintegration of nature. When Arnold tries to be most like the romantic poets, as in the pastiche of Keats in 'The Scholar-Gipsy', he is really least like them, in spite of his attempt to show the 'interinanimation' of natural things. The esemplastic force sweeping through nature in the romantic vision has fled away and left dry isolated husks behind. In Arnold's hands nature poetry becomes like descriptions in a botanical handbook—accurate, but superficial:

> Through the thick corn the scarlet poppies peep,
> And round green roots and yellowing stalks I see
>     Pale pink convolvulus in tendrils creep;
>         And air-swept lindens yield
> Their scent, and rustle down their perfumed showers
>     Of bloom on the bent grass where I am laid . . .

If nature is just a collection of things, it is hopeless to seek any spiritual presence there which might be a support for man. Imitating nature or seeking harmony with nature no longer means trying to plunge our roots, like nature's, in the ground of the absolute, or trying, through atunement with nature, to reach that ground. Each man must imitate nature in her mute acceptance of separation from God, and be like a stone, rounded in upon himself, with a stone's independence and persistence in being itself. Joy comes not from participation in the general life, but from a blind perseverance in performing the acts appropriate to our own natures. The stars and the sea are 'Bounded by themselves, and unregardful/In what state God's other works may be' and they 'demand not that the things without them/Yield them love, amusement, sympathy'. Yet they perform their appointed tasks with joy. Each man must also learn to be a law unto himself: 'To its own impulse every creature stirs;/Live by thy light, and earth will live by hers!'

This lesson of nature is really a lesson of despair, for though nature is to be admired for her ability to endure isolation, this calm self-enclosure, the satisfied peace of a rock merely being a rock, is impossible for man. Man's trouble is that he finds in himself no given law to direct his being. He desperately needs help from outside, someone or something to tell him what to do and who to be. Can nature do no more than bid man attempt something impossible? . . .

From Chapter 5 of *The Disappearance of God*, Harvard University Press, Cambridge, Mass., 1963, pp. 235–7.

# Arnold's Language - Some Views

## F. W. BATESON

### Victorian Poetic Language

... Tennyson did not try to write either in ignorance of or in indifference to the linguistic tendencies of his time. His poems are made out of the diction of the day—'the best words in the best order' that were then available, and his limited success serves to show up the failure of the other romantic poets of his generation. Tennyson was at least aware of the condition of the language he was compelled to use. His contemporaries, on the contrary, were *language-proof*. They bluntly refused to concern themselves with problems of diction and style. 'The poet', they would have agreed with Newman, 'is a compositor; words are his types; he must have them within reach, and in unlimited abundance.' And the consequence of this mechanical conception of composition was that, falling unconscious victims to the contradictory tendencies of the period, they cannot strictly be said to have a *style* at all. They have idiosyncrasies of expression; but that is another matter.

A theory of poetry that has no place for diction must offer something in its stead. The Victorians offered the subject. The romantic ideal of style was, as we have seen, 'something which must derive its poetic validity entirely from the matter committed to it'.[1] The earlier romantic poets had derived this matter from the subconscious mind. If they selected one subject rather than another, it was because some subjects will stimulate the subconscious mind more than others. They had not fallen into the mistake, into which the later poets fell, of considering some subjects essentially poetical. 'A great artist', Byron once said, 'will make a block of stone as sublime as a mountain, and a good poet can imbue a pack of cards with more poetry than inhabits the forests of America.'[2] With this dictum we may contrast Matthew Arnold's war-cry: 'All depends upon the subject; choose a fitting action, penetrate yourself with the feeling of its situations; this done, everything else will follow.'[3] The subject was the red herring of Victorian criticism, and many of the errors of that criticism—its neglect of Donne, its half-

---

[1] I have borrowed this excellent definition from Professor Lascelles Abercrombie's *Romanticism*, 1926, p. 25.

[2] *Letters and Journals*, ed. R. E. Prothero, Vol. 5, 1901, p. 557.

[3] 'Preface' (*Poems*, 1853).

heartedness to Blake, its disparagement of Shelley[4]—are directly traceable to its influence. But it would be incorrect to attribute all the deficiencies of the Victorian poets to the doctrine of the subject. The most that can be said is that it encouraged them in their habits of lin-- guistic indifference. The real case against mid-Victorian poetry, other than Tennyson's, is not that it rests upon a mistaken basis of theory but that it is badly written.

The example of Matthew Arnold is especially instructive because Arnold was not naturally a poet but a man of letters. His place is with such writers as Addison and Goldsmith, and Mr Aldous Huxley to-day —writers who, one feels, at whatever period they happen to be born, *must* express themselves through literature, though the particular literary form they may select is ultimately immaterial and dependent on the fashion of the moment. Poetry happened to possess more prestige than any other form in the mid-nineteenth century, and Arnold wrote poems. But I can find no trace in all his intelligent and readable verse of any specifically poetic originality. The sensibility reflected in it is not that of Arnold himself but of his age, and the style is an amalgam of the language that was then available for poetry. And what language it was!

> And Wordsworth! Ah, pale Ghosts, rejoice!
> For never has such soothing voice
> Been to your shadowy world convey'd,
> Since erst, at morn, some wandering shade
> Heard the clear song of Orpheus come
> Through Hades, and the mournful gloom.

Apart from the vicious exclamations—a pet trick of Arnold's, like the forcible-feeble use of italics, and both traceable to a desperate effort to impart an artificial emphasis to a naturally unemphatic diction—was it necessary to describe *Ghosts* as *pale*? If Hades is populated by wandering *shades* need we be told that it is *shadowy*? Is not *gloom* always *mournful*? And logical confusion is added to the redundancy. Wordsworth's *soothing* voice is compared to Orpheus's *clear* song. But why, especially in the gloom of Hades, should a clear song be soothing? One would have imagined that it would be more likely to be disturbing. What finally is the significance of *at morn*? Is not Hades always equally dark? Or, if there are gradations of light, are we to visualize the relative darkness or the relative brightness of morning?

The passage I have quoted is not in the least exceptional. Read hurriedly it is not unimpressive. But once it is subjected to a critical scrutiny the vagueness of its diction and the looseness of its thought are inescapable. The words are the ghosts of words. Two words have to be used to do the work of one. And the trickle of meaning is obscured in a

---

[4] Palgrave's *Golden Treasury* omits Donne and Blake altogether. Arnold ('Byron' in *Essays in Criticism, Second Series*) detected in Shelley 'the incurable want of a sound subject-matter'—an opinion shared by Patmore (*Principle in Art*, 1890, p. 114).

fog of associations conjured up by the implied reference to parallel passages in the *Odyssey,* the *Georgics,* and the *Aeneid.* It would be unfair, however, to lay all the blame on Arnold, who merely accepted the style and the language current in his time. It is the limitations of that style and that language, especially in conjunction, that I wish to emphasize. . . .

From *English Poetry and the English Language,* Oxford University Press, 1934, pp. 104–7. One footnote has been omitted.

## GEORGE H. FORD
### Arnold and Keats

. . . A large part of Arnold's verse exemplifies the theory of style which he expounded to Clough and to the English public at large. I do not mean that he ever achieved the 'grand style' (in the sense which he used that phrase), although he made strong efforts to do so in 'Sohrab and Rustum,' an Homeric imitation of which he was very proud. But in many poems he did achieve what we might call an anti-Keatsian style, a style from which Keatsian exuberance has been almost entirely chastened. We may consider such poems before passing on to those which are much closer to Keats.

Perhaps the most outstanding feature of Arnold's chastening of style is his minimization of sensuousness. Not only is there a complete dearth of tactile and olfactory sensations (which his contemporary, Baudelaire, was exploiting in every possible direction), but colour itself is almost entirely absent. Lafcadio Hearn goes so far as to say that the poems are simply 'colourless'. In such typical pieces as 'Memorial Verses' or 'To Marguerite', one is a long way from the world of dazzling colours which Keats had employed so lavishly. As Trilling notes, Arnold does achieve a certain warm grey tone at times, and he is often successful with moonlight effects, as in 'Mycerinus':

> While the deep-burnish'd foliage overhead
> Splinter'd the silver arrows of the moon.

But the great world of colour, as we find it in 'The Eve of St Mark' or the 'Ode to a Nightingale' is one upon which Matthew Arnold seldom draws. Many of the poems, especially those of the 1867 volume, will illustrate F. L. Lucas' remark that Arnold 'tended to prefer sackcloth to satin', and that often his 'bareness becomes threadbare'. Such jerky pieces as the 'Epilogue to Lessing's Laocoön' or 'Heine's Grave', whatever their virtues as criticism, are of a baldness which makes even the style of Wordsworth seem blazing with colours by comparison.

One hardly needs to quote from these poems to illustrate the point. Any lines selected at random will serve. A better example is such a piece as 'The Strayed Reveller' where certain concessions are made to the pictorial sense:

See, how glows,
Through the delicate flush'd marble,
The red creaming liquor,
Strown with dark seeds!

Arnold seems almost Keatsian here, but if the poem is more closely
examined, a striking difference is to be noted. The short line (of which
he was so fond) eliminates the tendency to develop metaphor and simile.
I have referred earlier to some resemblance between the theme of this
poem and Keats's 'Hyperion'. We may note also a certain similarity in
details. Keats had written:

As when, upon a tranced summer-night,
Those green-rob'd senators of mighty woods,
Tall oaks, branch-charmed by the earnest stars,
Dream, and so dream all night without a stir. . . .

Arnold's lines are:

Ah cool night-wind, tremulous stars!
Ah glimmering water—
Fitful earth-murmur—
Dreaming woods!

The two passages are more interesting in their divergencies than in any
likeness which they share. Arnold chooses to do without the richness of
imagery, and here as elsewhere in such poems, subordinates his colours
as he advocated in the 1853 Preface. It is, in fact, much closer to sculpture than to painting, and a type of sculpture very different from that
sometimes employed by Keats. In 'Hyperion' the delineation of the
great figures of the fallen Titans has all the massiveness of Michel-
angelo. Arnold's sculpture is on a different scale. As Quiller-Couch
observes, his poetry leaves the impression of something done in 'low
relief'.

The theme of 'The New Sirens' confirms, I think, this general
impression. Arnold could be tempted, as the Obermann poems show,
by the world of the romantic retreat. And 'The New Sirens' demonstrates that he was sometimes attracted to an indulgence of the
passions à la Byron. But he does not speak in his poems of the Lotos-
land of sensuousness as an alternative worthy to sway him from the
paths of a dedicated life. The comparative plainness of style in most of
his poetry corroborates what seems to have been a bent of his own
nature.

If, in the sphere of word-painting Arnold seems to be in reaction
against Keats, in that of verse-music he seems to be in reaction against
Tennyson. Keats's charming smoothness of style had been extensively
developed by the poet-laureate. The success of such a poem as 'The
Lotos-Eaters' in its manipulation of dulcet sounds into perfect harmony
became, for the Victorian reader, the very standard of excellence.

Matthew Arnold refused to conform. Through all his experiments with metrical forms he was working along his own lines, not in the direction of smoother melodies but towards a simpler, more intellectualized conversational style, and, it may be added, away from Keats and Tennyson. As Trilling remarks, his poetry has certain affinities with the 'iron harmonies', the dissonance of John Donne, rather than with the 'golden singers' of the stamp of Keats. The comparative absence of melody, together with the want of suggestiveness in pictorial image, gives his style an air of asceticism which is at the opposite pole from that of 'The Eve of St Agnes'.

In view of the Keatsian vogue in the later Victorian age, it was not unnatural that Arnold's stylistic methods would be little understood by his contemporaries. A reviewer of 1867, in comparing Arnold with Tennyson, grants the palm to the latter for the following reasons:

> . . . in variation of softly brilliant, exquisitely appropriate imagery, picture after picture of breathing, ruddy-tinted life, each picture speaking forth the argument in glow of noblest colour, each picture moving on as in rhythmic starry dance to the music of the whole,— the . . . poetry of Tennyson has the everlasting and incomparable superiority.[1]

Each one of these epithets is revealing. Keats's lessons had been learned only too well by the generations which succeeded his own, and Arnold's efforts to rectify the convention would hardly be appreciated. If that stylistic reformer had read the review, however, he would merely have shrugged. He was content to rest his case in another court. 'My poems', he said, 'represent . . . the main movement of mind of the last quarter of a century, and thus they will probably have their day. . . .'

On the other hand, if Arnold had chosen to reply to the review, taking examples from a restricted group of his own poems, he might have been able to challenge comparison with the followers of Keats on their own ground. He might, for example, have cited the case of his 'Scholar-Gipsy' with its succession of striking vignettes and its Keatsian stanza form:

> Shepherds had met him on the Hurst in spring;
> At some lone alehouse in the Berkshire moors,
> On the warm ingle bench, the smock-frock'd boors
> Had found him seated at their entering. . . .

For Arnold, in spite of all his protests against the influence of Keats's style, did not succeed in remaining completely immune himself. A group of his poems bear the unmistakable stamp of the earlier artist. This group includes some of his very finest work: 'Thyrsis', 'The Scholar-Gipsy' and 'Tristram and Iseult'. . . .

[1] Peter Bayne, 'Mr Arnold and Mr Swinburne', *The Contemporary Review*, Vol. 4, 1867, p. 356.

From Chapter 7 of *Keats and the Victorians*, Yale University Press, New Haven, Conn., 1944, pp. 78–81. Some footnotes have been omitted.


## R. A. FOAKES

### The Rhetoric of Assertion

. . . What affirmation there is in Arnold's poetry seems unimportant because it lacks the glow and thrill of the Romantic assertion; it provides a sad substitute for the vision of love in a 'struggling task'd morality', with its ideal of self-control, self-dependence, and release from passion. This is imaged in calm moonlight, the independent stillness of the stars, the calm motion of the sea: whatever token utterances he made occasionally to the contrary, his desire was not for involvement with the one life in and around us, but for withdrawal from that involvement in life which he felt to be necessary, and yet unavailing in his 'iron age'.

> We, in some unknown Power's employ,
> Move on a rigorous line;
> Can neither when we will, enjoy,
> Nor, when we will, resign.

'Fate drives me', he says, back from Obermann's world to his own course of life, where he is caught

> Wandering between two worlds, one dead,
> The other powerless to be born,
> With nowhere yet to rest my head.

The world of faith, of the vision of unity, of joy, is dead, and nothing has replaced it; all that remains is the desire to resign, to escape from the 'hot prison', the restlessness, the pain of life, into stillness like that of the stars or the sea, 'self-pois'd'.

It is not surprising then that his language proves often inadequate, especially in the rhetoric of assertion and the rhetoric of love. The vocabulary has become hollow, and is not supported by the imagery or the general tone of the poetry. Sometimes the effect is almost bathetic:

> Sink, O youth, in thy soul!
> Yearn to the greatness of Nature;
> Rally the good in the depths of thyself!

The image of the buried life in Arnold's poetry is effective as a type of the inaccessibility of the unifying vision, and conflicts here with the vocabulary of assertion: it is traditional to look upwards in aspiration, to seek good in the heights and evil in the depths. The idea of sinking in these lines is at odds with the idea of yearning to greatness, and their feebleness is due to this. Sometimes a clumsy vagueness of language and avoidance of the obvious and most compelling words, reduce the assertion to triviality:

> Unquiet souls!
> —In the dark fermentation of earth,
> In the never idle workshop of nature,
> In the eternal movement,
> Ye shall find yourselves again!

It is not pleasant to dwell on what happens to the dead in the 'workshop of nature', and this image conflicts with, rather than prepares for, the last two lines, which remain meaningless.

An inadequacy of language appears in many other passages of assertion. Often there is a kind of contradiction within the assertion, which seems to be withdrawn even as it is made. So for instance in 'Obermann Once More', the poet-recluse who speaks to Arnold in a vision ends his message on a note of optimism,

> The world's great order dawns in sheen,
> After long darkness rude,
> Divinelier imaged, clearer seen,
> With happier zeal pursued.

He urges Arnold to use his powers to help men to attain joy, to 'tell Hope to a world new-made'; but between the statement that a new order has burst forth, and the exhortation, three stanzas intervene describing Arnold as joyless, powerless, old, 'dimm'd' and weak, and it seems hardly possible that this man should be the prophet of new hope, while

> round thy firmer manhood cast,
> Hang weeds of our sad time.

The word 'weeds' had been used in connection with Obermann in 'Stanzas from the Grande Chartreuse',

> The world, which for an idle day
> Grace to your mood of sadness gave,
> Long since hath flung her weeds away.

Here the sense is clear, and the word can only refer to clothes; but in 'Overmann Once More', the meaning is confused, partly because the context limits it less precisely, partly because the word has already appeared in the poem in a quite different sense. The impact on the western world of Christianity is described by the visionary Overmann in terms of relief at the discovery of a solace for the spiritual desert of life; he says of the 'victorious West',

> 'Mid weeds and wrecks she stood—a place
> Of ruin—but she smiled!

'Weeds of our sad time' seems to carry overtones of this, to suggest ruin, a wilderness, as well as clothes. Perhaps this is merely fanciful, but the contrast and implicit conflict between the new world dawning in brightness, 'clearer seen', and its prophet, sad, joyless, and 'dimm'd', is apparent.

Sometimes there is an uncertainty in the phrasing of the assertion, and the lack of conviction in the utterance reduce or destroys its force. One form this uncertainty takes is the use of a modifying 'haply', 'may', or some such means of withdrawing from a commitment to a belief; so 'The Future' ends with the hope that

> Haply the river of Time . . .
> May acquire, if not the calm
> Of its early mountainous shore,
> Yet a solemn peace of its own;

and 'The Buried Life', after describing the rare moments when 'a lost pulse of feeling stirs again', and the poet finds release from the burden of life in the revelation of a nobler, inward life, moments when 'the heart lies plain', ends by implying that the revelation may be an illusion after all, as the word 'thinks' cancels the certainty:

> And then he thinks he knows
> The hills where his life rose,
> And the sea where it goes.

Another form of uncertainty appears in 'A Wish', in which the poet asks that on his deathbed he may become one with the universe and feel 'The pure eternal course of life'; but this ennobling vision of becoming 'wed' in soul to the everlasting

> world which was ere I was born,
> The world which lasts when I am dead,

is suddenly dropped at the end of the poem, where, instead of the glow of a release into a new unity, the transfiguration which might be expected as a climax, there is simply resignation to the doubt of 'To work *or* wait elsewhere *or* here':

> Thus feeling, gazing, might I grow
> Compos'd, refresh'd ennobled, clear;
> Then willing let my spirit go
> To work or wait elsewhere or here!

Perhaps a less obvious way in which an assertion is weakened is in a confusion or vagueness of ideas or in a syntactical obscurity. An instance may be found in 'Rugby Chapel',

> See! In the rocks of the world
> Marches the host of mankind,
> A feeble wavering line.

Where are they tending?—A God
Marshall'd them, gave them their goal.

In this image as it relates to its context there is a double ambiguity. It is part of the image of the journey of life on which the whole poem is based; the course of most men has been described as 'an eddy of purposeless dust', and the few who, like the poet, seek to advance to 'a clear-purposed goal' are set off from the crowd, in their lonely, difficult journeying. Yet now, towards the end of the poem, the 'host of mankind' suddenly appears to be engaged on the same journey as the few, a transference perhaps reflected in the contrast between the images of a marching host and a 'feeble wavering line'. The host, whose lives had been described as 'without aim', are now also suddenly given an aim, not one of their own choosing, but one prescribed by 'A God'; great souls like the poet's father have been called a few lines earlier, 'Servants of God', and the question arises, are these the same God? It would seem not, for the great souls are dedicated to the Christian God, whereas the other God represents merely a kind of fate, pushing men through life. This passage illustrates the rhetorical jugglery in which Arnold became involved when he sought to crown a poem expressing a melancholy view of life in his time with an ending of assertion which is not fully supported by the main theme; the cry

On, to the bounds of the waste,
On, to the City of God,

rings a little hollow after the terrible picture drawn in the first 130 lines of the poem. In the same way, the note of optimism at the end of 'A Summer Night',

How fair a lot to fill
Is left to each man still!

is not really supported by the main body of the poem; this describes two ways of life, that of the majority, a meaningless, prison-like existence, and that of 'the rest', who seek contact with the eternal, but disappear in the search for a 'false, impossible shore'; these two ways account for all men, and the transference to an assertive ending is achieved only by means of an apostrophe to the heavens, which are doubtfully and vaguely drawn into an association with man's life, for they

though so noble, share in the world's toil,
And, though so task'd keep free from dust and soil!
I will not say that your mild deeps retain
A tinge, it may be, of their silent pain
Who have long'd deeply once, and long'd in vain—
But I will rather say that you remain
A world above man's head, to let him see
How boundless might his soul's horizons be . . .

The heavens thus become an example for man, and seem to offer a third way of life ('How good it were to abide there . . .'); but it is not clear how they 'share in the world's toil', and the assertion that they are involved in human suffering is characteristically withdrawn even as it is made, in the phrase 'I will *not* say that. . .'.

An inadequacy of language is also seen in the intrusion on a number of occasions of a *deus ex machina* in the person of Fate, or of a god which is the equivalent of fate. This offered the poet a tactic for evading issues raised in his poems, and helped him sometimes to slip into an assertive ending not fully justified by the rest of the poem, as noted above in the case of 'Rugby Chapel', at other times to avoid making the assertion demanded by the rest of the poem. The most prominent example of this is in the Marguerite poems; in 'Meeting' the poet is about to leap ashore to welcome her, his 'bliss', but instead of the expected culmination, there is a sudden transposition to a language that would have been appropriate in some early eighteenth-century poetry; accents which might have sounded well in *The Rape of the Lock* seem strangely out of key here:

> I know that graceful figure fair,
> That cheek of languid hue;
> I know that soft, enkerchief'd hair,
> And those sweet eyes of blue.
>
> Again I spring to make my choice;
> Again in tones of ire
> I hear a God's tremendous voice:
> 'Be counsell'd, and retire.'

This failure of language in the rhetoric of assertion and the rhetoric of love reflects the most terrible feature of Arnold's poetry, the disintegration of the Romantic vision. A struggling task'd morality is substituted for the vision of love, an image of absolute peace in isolation; and the vision of the one life within us and abroad is replaced by the ideal of the self-dependent single life, calm and free from passion. . . .

From *The Romantic Assertion: a Study in the Language of Nineteenth-Century Poetry*, Methuen, 1958, pp. 159–65.


## CHRISTOPHER RICKS

### Verbal Achievement is an Essential Issue

[Professor Ricks was reviewing *Matthew Arnold: a Study of the Aesthetic Temperament in Victorian England* by W. A. Madden, and *Matthew Arnold: the Poet as Humanist* by G. R. Stange, both published in 1967.]

... Both Mr Stange and Mr Madden are scrupulous historians of culture; both make relevant and important historical points; but both fail to engage vigorously with the poetry because both find themselves without the space or the will or the focus which would encourage them to get down to that close verbal criticism essential to vivid literary studies. Not that all literary criticism demands the same degree of verbal criticism, and I appreciate that an undertaking such as Mr Madden's or Mr Stange's is different from any that I have ever tried. Yet it may be that there is an irreducible minimum of detailed and argued contact with the words of the poem, without which the criticism ceases to be itself. If there is one thing you can't do with poems, it is take them as read.

This is not to say that the case against Arnold's poetry adumbrated by Dr Leavis (that he was a very intelligent man who succumbed to faded poetic conventions, and whose *words* have no grip) is now the patent and substantiated truth. The point is that no writer on Arnold can afford either to ignore or to make merely rhetorical concessions towards such a critical point of view. Arnold's phrasing does not have unquestioned authority. Admittedly, it would be a great inconvenience to Mr Stange's argument, or Mr Madden's, if at every point they had to make manifest to us the *poetic* authority of the verse which they quote, and it is not surprising that they often hurry on. Which is why it would demand heroically diverse powers in a critic to be able to do justice to both the poetry and the 'ideas'. The sad fact is that unless justice (not to be confused with mercy) is done towards the poetry, the ideas become impalpable ubiquitous things ('for things are bad all over, etc., etc.').

Take some passages from Arnold quoted either by Mr Madden or Mr Stange. The question is simply whether they have so indisputable an authority of phrasing as to allow any critic not to deal with the question of whether they are well *written*. When Arnold thinks of the earth and invokes 'The tribes who then roam'd on her breast' ('The Future'), what is there in the poem which makes 'breast 'into anything more than a cliché? Would not 'roaming' be unseemly or ludicrous if it were not that no reader imagines the breast with any immediacy? (The same is true of Tennyson's vacant line, 'And the lake's gloomy bosom is full to the brim'.)

When in 'The Scholar-Gipsy' the scholar is 'tired of knocking at preferment's door', why is Arnold not merely living off Swift ('They crowd about Preferment's gate') or off Johnson ('Unnumber'd suppliants crowd Preferment's gate')? On the face of it, Arnold's wording is full of clichés; perhaps they are clichés newly used and renovated, but that would need to be argued for. Not to mention such things at all is to be in collusion with one's poet. Take the well-known praise of Wordsworth in 'Memorial Verses':

> The cloud of mortal destiny
> Others will front it fearlessly—
> But who, like him, will put it by?

Fronting a cloud is not a clear process; more important, it is not self-evidently a brave thing to do. What is fearless about fronting a cloud? And what would it be to 'put' a cloud 'by'? Again, the point is not that no answers could be given to such questions; it is that unless the standing of Arnold's metaphors is genuinely considered, the words are merely words upon the topmost froth of thought.

Mr Stange remarks upon how the New Sirens 'celebrate the Romantic cult of feeling and the supremacy of the heart over the head' (p. 46), and he quotes:

'Come', you say, 'the brain is seeking,
While the sovran heart is dead;
Yet this glean'd, when Gods were speaking,
Rarer secrets than the toiling head'.

Is 'brain' then simply interchangeable with 'head'? If so, the phrasing is slack; if not, then it is hard to see what distinction Arnold is making (and Mr Stange makes no comment).

The poet who sings them may die,
But they are immortal and live . . .

If they are immortal, they live; that much we could not but have deduced for ourselves. Perhaps Arnold is making some subtle point by his phrasing; if not (and the critic is silent), his phrasing on the face of it would seem wordy.

Naturally, neither Mr Madden nor Mr Stange makes out that Arnold is a faultless poet but neither of them meets the disobliging fact that the verbal achievement is an essential issue whenever a poem is quoted. . . .

From *Victorian Studies*, Vol. 11, 1968, pp. 539–45 (541–3).

# The Man and the Poet -
# a Summing up

... Integration—this is the obsessive theme of Arnold's youthful letters to Clough, the integration of the individual, the integration of the work of art, the integration, finally, of the social order. Paradoxically, Arnold sought the way to his own personal integration through an Elizabethan eccentricity of conduct. In the end, however, the fate he feared and fought overtook him; the poetic power passed away. It passed with youth and the ability to maintain the youthful dandyism. He was always to retain a reasoned admiration of gaiety and high spirits, and a light insouciance to use against the pointless sobriety of English culture; he was everlastingly elegant and perhaps not annoyed at being called a Jeremiah in kid gloves. But the youthful quality which had sustained his poetry disappears.

He seems always, in the Romantic fashion, to have been awaiting its inevitable end. Few poets can have been more conscious of their youth. 'But be bustling about it; we are growing old, and advancing towards the deviceless darkness: it would be well not to reach it till we had at least tried *some* of the things men consider desirable.' The theme recurs so often. 'How life rushes away, and youth. One has dawdled and scrupled and fiddle faddled—and it is all over.' 'What a difference there is between reading in poetry and morals of the loss of youth, and experiencing it!'

The tone of the gloriously excited letters to Clough becomes calmer and sinks to the flat, almost desperate, coolness of the letters which G. W. E. Russell edited—letters so dull that their appearance after Arnold's death, Gosse tells us, gave a severe setback to his enviable reputation[1]. Arnold became the man whom Jowett was to praise by saying that 'he was the most sensible man of genius whom I have ever known and the most free from personality'. Arnold of the untrimmed hair[2] and the gay waistcoats, the elaborate hoaxes and the flourishing opinion! He himself knows it. 'I am past thirty', he says, 'and three parts iced over.'

---

[1] The opinion of Arnold Bennett dissents charitably: 'His letters make very good quiet reading.'

[2] He never lost his pride in his hair, however: 'that perpetual miracle, my hair', he said, and he offered to let a friend pull it to scotch any suspicion that it might be a wig.

He himself knows it and with the utmost pain. He is frozen over but he is fearfully conscious of what lies beneath the ice. He is reconciled, he would have himself believe, to the course of his life; for there is, he fancies hesitantly, a power which, by shaping the impulses even against our conscious will, works out to the individual's good, even though, to him, it does not seem good. And yet

. . . Often, in the world's most crowded streets,
But often, in the din of strife,
There rises an unspeakable desire
After the knowledge of our buried life,
A thirst to spend our fire and restless force
In tracking out our true, original course;
A longing to inquire
Into the mystery of this heart that beats
So wild, so deep in us, to know
Whence our thoughts come and where they go.
And many a man in his own breast then delves,
But deep enough, alas, none ever mines:
And we have been on many thousand lines,
And we have shown on each talent and power,
But hardly have we, for one little hour,
Been on our own line, have we been ourselves.

He is only forty-five when his last volume appears. It is very slim, though it is the product of fifteen years. It is very admirable, but undoubtedly, as Arnold himself says, the Muse has gone away. The poet looks back to 'the joy, the bloom, the power' and after this volume he writes no more poetry in the twenty-one years that yet remain to him. But in 1849 he is twenty-seven and still joyous and his friends are puzzled by *The Strayed Reveller* that has just appeared.

From Chapter 1 of *Matthew Arnold*, Columbia University Press, New York, and George Allen and Unwin, London, 2nd edition, 1949, pp. 33-5.

A. DWIGHT CULLER

# The World of the Poems

. . . The central feature of Arnold's world is a river which the poet unabashedly calls the River of Life or of Time. Characteristically, this river takes its rise in some cool glade on a high mountain, flows down through a gorge onto a hot and dusty plain, and then, after almost losing itself in the sands of the desert, empties at last into the full and glimmering sea. Needless to say, there are many variations upon this scene, and the one essential thing is that there should be three distinct regions which are separated from one another by some kind of 'gorge'. Borrowing phrases which Arnold himself employs, we may call these regions the Forest Glade, the Burning or Darkling Plain, and the Wide-Glimmering Sea. In the poem 'The Future', which is Arnold's most straightforward exposition of the River, these regions are identified with the past, the present, and the future, and that is generally the case when the River denotes historic time. More frequently, however, it denotes the life of the individual, and then the three regions are childhood, maturity, and old age or death. Whichever they be, they invariably have the same character: the first is a period of joyous innocence when one lives in harmony with nature, the second a period of suffering when one is alone in a hostile world, and the third a period of peace in which suffering subsides into calm and then grows up into a new joy, the joy of active service in the world.

The basis for this view is found in a conception of history which was widespread in Arnold's day. It was put forward by Herder, Goethe, and Novalis in Germany, by the Saint-Simonians in France, and by Carlyle in England. Carlyle's *French Revolution* presupposes it, and his *Sartor Resartus* sets it forth in personal terms. Diogenes Teufelsdröckh moves from childhood faith and joy, through the interregnum of the Everlasting No and Centre of Indifference, to the mature faith of the Everlasting Yea. Similarly, Arnold, in 'Stanzas from the Grande Chartreuse', represents himself as

Wandering between two worlds, one dead,
The other powerless to be born.

According to all these writers, this threefold pattern of history arose from the alternation of vital or organic periods, which are periods of faith and imagination, with mechanical or critical periods, which are periods of scepticism dominated by the understanding. (Arnold in 'The Function of Criticism at the Present Time' calls them 'epochs of expansion' and 'epochs of concentration'.) Actually, however, a later vital period never simply repeated an earlier one but rather incorporated into itself the lesson of the intervening critical period. Thus the total pattern was always a threefold cycle of thesis, antithesis, and synthesis, repeating itself over and over again. In 'Westminster Abbey' Arnold presupposes that the cycles will go on ascending forever, and in 'Obermann Once More' he sees a series of them in the past. But in general, the poem 'The Future' is right in assuming that a particular individual never takes in more than a single cycle of three, and that for him these are the past, the present, and the future. The present is always mechanical because this is the kind of theory of history that arises in mechanical periods. It declares that things were better in the past and that they will be better again in the future. In other words, it is the historical equivalent of the tragic view of life. As such, it is related to the great tragic patterns of the past—the cycle of birth, death, and rebirth which was the basis of Greek tragedy, and the cycle of Paradise, the expulsion from Paradise, and the 'Paradise within thee, happier far', which is the substance of Christian myth. In Arnold's day the particular movements involved were the thesis of Romanticism, the antithesis of Utilitarianism, and the synthesis of Christian humanism.

Though we have called the three regions of Arnold's world the Forest Glade, the Burning or Darkling Plain, and the Wide-Glimmering Sea, it should be understood that Arnold's symbols sometimes take forms not actually denoted by these names. He has, for example, a minor but pervasive ship-and-sea symbolism which is quite distinct from his symbolism of river and land. Nonetheless, it has the same structure and conveys a similar meaning. For his image of the Sea of Life (not to be confused with the sea into which the River of Life flows, which is more nearly a Sea of Death) is precisely comparable to the darkling plain. In one poem he even calls it the 'watery plain'. Further, there is an undersea world, consisting of 'kind sea-caves' and coral halls, which has the same remote, pastoral character as the forest glade. The fullest development of this is in 'The Forsaken Merman', but there are also suggestions of it in the Eaglehurst poem, the sonnet 'Written in Butler's Sermons', and 'To Marguerite—Continued'. And finally, parallel to the wide-glimmering sea is an alternative symbol for the third phase of life which we may call the City of God or Throne of Truth. This region, which is placed on high and is reached by strenuous effort, not by drifting down a stream, is very different in its implications from the wide-glimmering sea. Indeed, the alternatives are probably related to those of mountain glen and coral hall in the first phase of the myth, and whether one proceeds out of the deep unto the deep or out of the heavens unto the heavens are alternatives that Arnold kept open in his mind. In the early poem 'In Utrumque Paratus' he speculates that life may have originated in the depths, in the fecund body of Nature, or on the heights, in the pure mind of God, and he is 'ready for either alternative'—*in utrumque paratus.*

The first region of Arnold's world is usually presented as a place of deep or variegated shadow, cool and well-watered, with clear-running streams or bubbling fountains. Usually it is set on the shoulder of a mountain, but it may be in the corner of an upland field or in some sun-dappled meadow deep in the woods. It may even be on an open heath so that it is screened by trees or protected by some depression in the land. For its main characteristic, apart from the springlike and virginal quality of its vegetation, is that it is secluded from the world, withdrawn and remote, and that the persons who inhabit it, who are mostly youths and children, live there in pristine innocence, untroubled by the problems which will later shake them in the world.

The principal examples of this glade in Arnold's poetry are the 'queen's secluded garden' in which Sohrab was raised as a child, the 'green circular hollow in the heath' in which the children of Tristram and Iseult listen to their mother's story, and 'the last/Of all the woody, high, well-water'd dells/On Etna', of which Callicles sings to Empedocles. Standing for them all might be that in 'Stanzas from the Grande Chartreuse' in which the poet, taunted with his unfitness for the world, replies,

> We are like children rear'd in shade
> Beneath some old-world abbey wall,
> Forgotten in a forest-glade,
> And secret from the eyes of all,
> Deep, deep the greenwood round them waves,
> Their abbey, and its close of graves!

Even Oxford, as described in the *Essays in Criticism*, 'steeped in sentiment as she lies, spreading her gardens to the moonlight. and whispering from her towers the last enchantments of the Middle Age', is essentially a forest glade.

In its early stages the glade is intensely feminine and maternal. Indeed, the undersea world of 'The Forsaken Merman' is distinctly a womblike place in which children and other fishlike creatures float about in a brine until at last, rejected by their mother, they come to the surface, crying and 'wild with pain'. Not so deeply primitive are the other uses of the symbol, but, in their use of geological images and a subtle incest theme, they still suggest a Freudian unconscious or a time prior to individuation. In the sonnet 'Written in Butler's Sermons' it is said,

> Deep and broad, where none may see,
> Spring the foundations of that shadowy throne
> Where man's one nature, queen-like, sits alone,
> Centred in a majestic unity;
> And rays her powers, like sister-islands seen
> Linking their coral arms under the sea.

Similarly, in 'To Marguerite—Continued' it is asserted that although on the surface we are islands, 'Surely once . . . we were/Parts of a single continent!' and this is further evidenced by the fact that underneath the sea the islands are connected with one another by a deep volcanic fire. So, too, in 'Empedocles on Etna' the Liparëan islands are connected with each other, and with Etna, by 'sister-fires', although on the surface they are connected only by 'a road of moonbeams'.

Putting behind us the undersea version of Arnold's world and coming up into its more normal pastoral form we find that it is still presided over by queens and mothers, ultimately by the Great or Mighty Mother, Nature. Gradually, however, as the children grow up, sisters and mothers are forgotten, and then it becomes a young man's world, in which youth ranges freely with his male companions. His activities are three: the hunt, love, and poetry or song. Love, however, quickly turns to sexual passion, which is a subject for the burning plain, and so the prime activities are the hunt and poetry or song.

The hunt is Arnold's main symbol for the active life in the world of nature. It is true that in 'Stanzas from the Grande Chartreuse' the children of the abbey were unable to follow the hunters, who symbolized to them the life of pleasure, and to the pure contemplatives of 'Thyrsis' and 'The Scholar-Gipsy' the troops of Oxford hunters somewhat disturbed the landscape with their clatter. But Rustum remembered with pleasure the life he led

>in that long-distant summer-time—
>The castle, and the dewy woods, and hunt
>And hound, and morn on those delightful hills
>In Ader-baijan.

Tristram was a 'peerless hunter' before his life was poisoned by Iseult of Ireland, and the young huntsman who stares down upon him from the arras is inclined to cheer his dogs into the brake (though 'the wild boar rustles in his lair') rather than linger in that world of heated passion. Both Æpytus in *Merope* and the Duke of Savoy in 'The Church of Brou' die in hunting accidents, the one pursuing the stag in Arcadian dales and the other pursuing the boar in the crisp woods of France. In both cases this is the crucial event which moves the action of the poem from one phase of life to another.

Tristram was both hunter and poet, as his gold harp and dark green forest-dress suggest, but generally in Arnold the poet roams the woodlands without hunting. In 'The Strayed Reveller' Ulysses hunted with Circe, but he is clearly to be contrasted with the more dreamy youth who, having descended from his hut up at the valley-head, merely sits on the steps and lets the forms of things pass through his mind rather than he through the forms. The youths who descend from the upland valleys to the palace of the New Sirens are poets, and so too are various figures in 'The Scholar-Gipsy', 'Thyrsis', and the lyrics of Callicles. Callicles himself is the best example, unless one excepts Wordsworth, who, in 'Memorial Verses', is primarily for Arnold a poet of the forest glade.

> He laid us as we lay at birth
> On the cool flowery lap of earth,
> Smiles broke from us and we had ease;
> The hills were round us, and the breeze
> Went o'er the sun-lit fields again;
> Our foreheads felt the wind and rain.
> Our youth return'd; for there was shed
> On spirits that had long been dead,
> Spirits dried up and closely furl'd,
> The freshness of the early world.

If one wanted a single line to express the character of the forest glade, it would be, 'The freshness of the early world'. If one wanted a single word, it would be that word, so important both to Romantic poetry and the poetry of Arnold—'Joy'. Joy is what the forest glade possessed and what the burning plain has lost.

The moment of transition between the forest glade and the burning plain—as also between the burning plain and the wide-glimmering sea—is what Arnold calls the Gorge. When he is using his ship-and-sea imagery, the gorge takes the form of a straight or narrows which the ship must negotiate to get from one body of water into another. We have examples in 'Stanzas from Carnac' and 'The Scholar-Gipsy'. When he is using the alternative image of the pilgrim and the City of God, it takes the form of a mountain pass or narrow defile. There are examples in 'Sohrab and Rustum', 'Balder Dead', and 'Rugby Chapel'. In 'Balder Dead' it also takes the form of the bridge and grate which have to be negotiated by the messenger Hermod in going from the world of the gods to the world of the dead. In poems which make use of the undersea world, it is the turbulent surf at the junction of sea and land. In 'The Forsaken Merman' the children have to go through this surf in passing from their coral halls to the windy shore, and in 'Dover Beach' it is 'the long line of spray/Where the sea meets the moon-blanch'd land', which separates the Sea of Faith from the darkling plain. In 'Stanzas in Memory of the Author of "Obermann" ' we are told that the modern generation was reared in hours

> Of change, alarm, surprise—
> What shelter to grow ripe is ours?
> What leisure to grow wise?
>
> Like children bathing on the shore,
> Buried a wave beneath,
> The second wave succeeds, before
> We have had time to breathe.

Finally, in Arnold's more usual symbolism the Gorge is an actual gorge in which the River of Life, foaming between black, threatening

cliffs, plunges in torrents down to the burning plain. There is something
of the same feeling that we get in Wordsworth's Simplon Pass passage,
of sick fear and giddy tumult, of noise and dark confusion, but for
Arnold it is a traumatic experience. In 'The Future' it is explicitly made
the end of the first phase of life:

> Where the snowy mountainous pass,
> Echoing the screams of the eagles,
> Hems in its gorges the bed
> Of the new-born clear-flowing stream.

In 'A Dream' we have an almost archetypal presentation of this moment.
'We sail'd, I thought we sail'd/ . . . down a green Alpine stream'. The
banks of the stream have all the sun-drenched beauty of the forest glade,
and on a balcony overlooking the stream are two girls, of whom the poet
says that 'more than mortal impulse fill'd their eyes'. The youths,
responding to this impulse, rose, then gazed:

> One moment, on the rapid's top, our boat
> Hung poised—and then the darting river of Life
> (Such now, methought, it was), the river of Life,
> Loud thundering, bore us by; swift, swift it foam'd,
> Black under cliffs it raced, round headlands shone.
> Soon the plank'd cottage by the sun-warm'd pines
> Faded—the moss—the rocks; us burning plains,
> Bristled with cities, us the sea received.

The burning plain, the second region of Arnold's world, is the very
antithesis of the forest glade. Far from being a place where one is united
with his mother, it is likely to be a place where, out of ignorance, he
fights with his father. For this reason it is often shrouded in darkness,
in fog or swirling sand. But whether it be represented as a bleak and
wintry upland or a hot and arid desert, it is always barren of vegetation.
Moreover, where the glade was an enclosed, protected place, the plain
is precariously open and exposed. It is the Victorian equivalent of the
Wasteland. As such, it is at once empty and terrifyingly full: the one
thing that it is not is harmoniously unified. For whereas in the forest
glade man was in union with God, nature, and his fellow man, here he is
abandoned by God, divorced from nature, and alienated from his fellow
man. What is more, he is alienated even from himself, as the symbol of
the river makes clear.

For when the River of Life flows down onto the burning plain, it is
immediately split into several channels. As Arnold says of the Oxus,

>                 then sands begin
> To hem his watery march, and dam his streams,
> And split his currents; that for many a league
> The shorn and parcell'd Oxus strains along
> Through beds of sand and matted rushy isles—

Oxus, forgetting the bright speed he had
In his high mountain-cradle in Pamere,
A foil'd circuitous wanderer—

These channels, one flowing out into the desert, another by a great city,
and another toward a grove of palms, are symbols of the partial and
fragmented lives which we lead as creatures of the plain. *Terrae filii* is
the name which Arnold gives them in his essays, and it is a name which
would well denote them here. Basically, they are three or four in number,
and since they are not really distinct persons, but rather roles which the
Youth is likely to take up in order, we may present them in a kind of
narrative of what happens to the Youth when he descends to the
burning plain.

His first reaction is one of anger. Looking around on the waste and
desolate scene, he is bitterly indignant that the world should be such a
place and that all his childhood dreams have been destroyed. And so,
railing harshly against the gods, he flings himself out into the desert and
races madly over the sands in the insane hope that there is some escape.
We see him in the daemonic questers in 'Resignation' and in the frail
figure clinging to the bark in 'A Summer Night'. Ultimately, of course,
he is shipwrecked, or sinks down exhausted, or loses his way, and at
this point he decides that he had better do as others have done before
him knuckle under and submit to the powers that be. And so he enters
one of the great cities which line the banks of the now sluggish river and
there gives himself to a life of 'quiet desperation'. In his first state
Arnold calls him a Madman, in his second he calls him a Slave.
Ostensibly, the two states are the very antithesis of each other, but
ultimately they are seen to be much the same. For the Madman is as
much a slave to his own passions as the Slave is to the world, and the
world is as arid and lonely a desert as the desert is itself. Therefore, the
poet cries,

Is there no life, but these alone?
Madman or slave, must man be one?

Yes, comes the answer, there are other lives than these, and among them
that of being unable to choose between Madman and Slave, and of
alternating fiercely between them. Tristram, torn between his two loves,
was such a person, and Empedocles, unable to live with men or with
himself, was another. Borrowing a name from the hero of Clough's
poem we may call him Dipsychus or the Divided Soul.

Confronted by this dilemma, the Youth is about to sink down in
despair when there meets his eyes, rising as a kind of mirage from the
desert, what seems to be an oasis and turns out to be a pleasure grove,
with a throng of noisy merry-makers, feasting and drinking far into the
night. To the Youth it looks as if these persons have created something
analogous to the forest glade, and such may have been their intention
when they began. But as he enters and joins with the throng, he soon
discovers that this grove is very different from that which he had known

as a child. The feminine figures are not those of mother and sister but
are languorous, seductive women—Circe, the New Sirens, Eugenia of
the 'Horatian Echo', and the Modern Sappho. Further, the buildings
of the grove are no longer the beloved abbeys and castles of his youth
but are classic palaces with porticos, balustrades, and marble columns.
Even the grove itself is false and metallic. In 'Mycerinus' 'the deep-
burnish'd foliage overhead / Splinter'd the silver arrows of the moon',
and a hundred lamps turned night into day. The spring or fountain,
which was the central feature of the forest glade, has now been replaced
by the foaming goblet or bowl, and it is from this source that the joy
of the Revellers (for so we may call them) flows. But their joy is not of
the kind that the Youth had previously known. Rather it is a hard,
mirthless laughter that is all too conscious of the desert just beyond the
trees and that quickly collapses into gloom. And this fierce alternation
between laughter and gloom  rapture and ennui, shows that by coming
into the grove the Youth has not escaped from the dilemma of Madman
and Slave but has merely transferred it to another situation.

Indeed, it is now clear to the Youth that the desert is not to be
avoided by any change of place but that he carries it with him wherever
he goes. And as he considers what has happened to the river of his life,
he sees that although on the surface it consists of thin and meagre
streams which wander across the desert, far beneath the surface there is
a subterranean river which flows, silent and strong, directly toward the
sea. This river—'The unregarded river of our life'—'The central stream
of what we feel indeed'—is Arnold's symbol of the Buried Life. Though
it constitutes our true or genuine self, we are for the most part unconscious of it while we are on the burning plain. But once we become
conscious of it, then there arises within us

> an unspeakable desire
> After the knowledge of our buried life; . . .
> A longing to inquire
> Into the mystery of this heart which beats
> So wild, so deep in us—to know
> Whence our lives come and where they go.
> ('The Buried Life', ll. 47–53).

For this purpose the Youth goes somewhat apart from the surface life
in which he is then engaged. If he is a Slave, he stands apart from the
world's work and becomes a Quietist. If he is a Madman, he pauses in
his wild career, ascends some eminence, and becomes a Sage. Or if he
is a Reveller, he wanders away from his companions into some quiet
part of the garden where, as a Strayed Reveller, he can commune with
his own soul.

> Sink, O youth, in thy soul!
> Yearn to the greatness of Nature;
> Rally the good in the depths of thyself!
> ('The Youth of Man', ll. 116–18).

The life of the Madman is imaged in Arnold by the straight-line movement of his flight, the life of the Slave by the circular movement of his treadmill existence within the city, the life of Dipsychus by the eddying or fluctuating movement of alternation, and the life of the Reveller by the sinuous movement among the palms. But the lives of Sage, Quietist, and Strayed Reveller are imaged by the still point, the moment of stasis, far above and yet plumbing far below the world's surface. Only at such moments and to such a point do there come, 'vague and forlorn, / From the soul's subterranean depth upborne', airs and floating echoes of our true or buried self. Arnold's poems mark the moments at which such echoes come. They are the times when he stands aside from his surface self and communes with his own soul. Initially, their aim is simply to intimate the existence of what cannot publicly be revealed, but ultimately it is to bring to the surface the buried self so that it may unite with the surface stream and flow, clear and whole, into the wide-glimmering sea.

The third phase of Arnold's myth, then, is the phase of reconciliation, first with the self and then with the world. The river joins its various streams and then it merges with the sea. As a result, the transition to the third phase is not ordinarily dramatic. Rather it is a moment of inward illumination in which, thinking that we are still in a desert, we suddenly discover that we are not, but are in a path leading to the City of God or in an estuary leading to the sea. These two places represent the alternative goals of Arnold's myth, and as we have already noted, they have very different implications. The one is religious, the other naturalistic. The one is to be gained by effort, the other without any effort at all. The one appears to be a final goal, with the suggestion that once it has been reached life's journey is done. The other is not so much a goal as a stage in the world-process, the great cyclical movement which Arnold calls 'the general life'. For although to man's limited vision the sea is death, to his more extended vision it is the All, the vast continuum of nature into which all things flow and out of which they again return. Finally, corresponding to these two goals are two characters who inhabit the third phase of Arnold's world. They are called the Servants or Sons of God and the Children of the Second Birth. At this point it is not necessary to say very much about them. The former are last seen making their way to the City of their Father, and the latter returning to the home of their mother. . . .

From the Introduction to *Imaginative Reason: the Poetry of Matthew Arnold*, Yale University Press, New Haven and London, 1966, pp. 3–16. Some footnotes have been omitted.

# *Dover Beach*

. . . 'Dover Beach' is quite free from any trace of poeticality. It is a short poem  but in it Arnold relates the symbolic landscape . . . to ideas which are also prominent elsewhere in his work. The general decline of faith and Arnold's own resultant bewilderment and melancholy constitute the theme of the 'Stanzas from the Grande Chartreuse'; in 'The Buried Life', Arnold expresses the belief that in a successful love-relationship he may discover certain values which are not readily to be found in 'modern life'. Both of these ideas reappear in 'Dover Beach'. . . .

The 'moon-blanch'd' landscape described in the opening lines is composed of details which suggest the serenity, balance, and stability which Arnold desired for himself. This setting is evoked with considerable vividness.

> The sea is calm to-night.
> The tide is full, the moon lies fair
> Upon the straits;—on the French coast the light
> Gleams and is gone; the cliffs of England stand,
> Glimmering and vast, out in the tranquil bay.
> Come to the window, sweet is the night-air!
> Only, from the long line of spray
> Where the sea meets the moon-blanch'd land,
> Listen! you hear the grating roar
> Of pebbles which the waves draw back, and fling,
> At their return, up the high strand,
> Begin, and cease, and then again begin,
> With tremulous cadence slow, and bring
> The eternal note of sadness in.

We can point to the steady and weighty *rallentando* with which the first sentence completes its series of affirmations; to the contrasting tender appeal of the invitation which follows; and to the richness and fullness with which the sound and movement of the sea are rendered in the concluding eight lines. Examining these lines more closely, we can cite 'grating roar' as admirably conveying the two distinguishable but inseparable sounds made by waves breaking on shingle; we can acknowledge the almost physical stress given to the verbs 'draw back' and 'fling'; we can analyse up to a point the combination of syntactical and metrical means by which the ebbing and flowing motion of the waves is made actual; and we can admire the appropriateness of the Miltonic 'tremulous cadence slow' both as summarizing what has gone before and as permitting an easy and natural introduction of the 'eternal note of sadness'. But with all such comments we are in danger of substituting convenient but arbitrary rationalizations and simplifications for the rich complexity of our experience while reading the poem. The least inadequate criticism of any poem will always be that implicit in a reading of it aloud to an understanding hearer. Formal literary analysis can offer only a few crude indications of what one would be trying to do when giving such a reading.

The image which dominates this first paragraph of 'Dover Beach' forms part of the 'full view' described by Mr W. H. Auden in his poem beginning, 'Look, stranger, on this island now'. Like Arnold, Mr Auden appears in his poetry as a tortured intellectual concerned with working out his own salvation. His inferior work, and his admirers' preference for it, gave him during the nineteen-thirties a reputation as a political poet. This was misleading. At his best, Mr Auden is a highly subjective poet; and like Arnold he tends to relate his mental states to symbolic landscapes. But, whereas Arnold's more successful landscapes seem to be apprehended by direct sensory experience, Mr Auden's consist largely of items culled from atlases, newsreels, the daily press, and political, psychological, and other reading. In short, his characteristic landscapes appear to be known to the intelligence rather than to the senses. This is exemplified at an extreme in 'Spain 1937' and in the verse 'Commentary' which concludes the sonnet-sequence 'In Time of War'. Admittedly, Mr Auden's early favourite landscape of industrial decay is sometimes rendered in potently sensuous terms; but this is unusual.

In the poem beginning, 'Look, stranger, on this island now', Mr Auden seems again to have made the unusual effort to impose the landscape he is describing upon the very senses of his readers. The result is a good poem; but it would have been a better poem if the effort had been less obtrusively visible. The second stanza is all that concerns us now:

> Here at the small field's ending pause
> When the chalk wall falls to the foam and its tall ledges
> Oppose the pluck
> And knock of the tide,
> And the shingle scrambles after the suck-
> -ing surf
> And the gull lodges
> A moment on its sheer side.

The internal rhymes and successive emphatic beats in the second line, the aggressively tactile and kinaesthetic images introduced by 'pluck' and 'knock' in the third and fourth, and the onomatopoeic splitting of the word 'sucking' between the fifth and sixth are effective devices but too deliberate. It is precisely the effortlessness, the confident ease of,

Arnold's description that is most remarkable when it is placed beside Mr Auden's. Arnold is doing supremely well what comes naturally to him; Mr Auden's description is, for him, a *tour de force*.

Having detected the 'eternal note of sadness', Arnold mentions a Sophoclean interpretation of it.

> Sophocles long ago
> Heard it on the Ægæan, and it brought
> Into his mind the turbid ebb and flow
> Of human misery; we
> Find also in the sound a thought,
> Hearing it by this distant northern sea.

The literary allusion serves not only to suggest that we have here to do with an archetypal image but also to introduce Arnold's own commentary.

This begins in a tone of straightforward exposition.

> The Sea of Faith
> Was once, too, at the full, and round earth's shore
> Lay like the folds of a bright girdle furl'd.

But instead of lapsing from this into rather flat rumination, which is what we have seen him do elsewhere, Arnold holds fast to the image of the sea. This has, so to speak, grown in his hands, so that it can now carry the whole weight of his feeling at the decline of religious faith. The symbol, so loaded, is presented in five haunting lines. The series of open vowels in the second of these, with the near-rhyme 'draw: roar', gives an eerie resonance which echoes down the remainder of the sentence with its 'falling' syntactical rhythm.

> But now I only hear
> Its melancholy, long, withdrawing roar,
> Retreating, to the breath
> Of the night-wind, down the vast edges drear
> And naked shingles of the world.

This is an early instance of the expressions of a horror of the utterly negative which occur from time to time in modern literature: in *A Passage to India* and *The Waste Land*, for example.

Critics acquainted with the extant manuscript of 'Dover Beach' sometimes complain that the last paragraph does not really belong with the remainder of the poem. In this draft, the last line is 'And naked shingles of the world. Ah love &c', which certainly suggests that the paragraph beginning 'Ah, love, let us be true' had already been written. But no amount of knowledge of its author's methods of composition can prove that a finished work is or is not a unified whole. With greater critical relevance, it may be argued that in this final paragraph Arnold has forgotten about the sea. But the sea has by this time served its purpose as a symbol; and that which it symbolized is still powerfully present in these last lines. Moreover, the darkness remains. Precisely because it is no longer possible to believe that the universe is in some degree adjusted to human needs, that it is informed by a divinity which sympathizes with men in their joys and sorrows and in their hopes and fears, the poet must seek in human love for those values which are undiscoverable elsewhere. Moreover—and this is the primary meaning of the last paragraph—the lovers must support each other if they are to live in the modern world without disaster.

> Ah, love, let us be true
> To one another! for the world, which seems
> To lie before us like a land of dreams,
> So various, so beautiful, so new,
> Hath really neither joy, nor love, nor light,
> Nor certitude, nor peace, nor help for pain;
> And we are here as on a darkling plain
> Swept with confused alarms of struggle and flight,
> Where ignorant armies clash by night.

As in the previous sentence, the main verb is introduced early; the result is what I have called a 'falling' syntactical rhythm, which contributes appreciably to the brooding melancholy of the whole paragraph. Metrically, this is the most regular section of the poem; after the initial short line, there are seven pentameters. The brief and therefore arresting last line carries the crucial phrase which discloses the full strangeness and horror of the concluding analogy. The

> darkling plain
> Swept with confused alarms of struggle and flight

is not remarkable; all the more powerful, therefore, is the harsh and surprising revelation, in the curtailed last line, of the nature of the battle: 'Where ignorant armies clash by night'. This image is Arnold's most impressive and most pregnant poetic utterance on 'modern life'.

'Dover Beach' is, I believe, his one great poem. As far as it is possible for a single short lyric to do so, it represents 'the main movement of mind of the last quarter of a century'; and it is the one work by Arnold which ought to appear in even the briefest anthology of great English poems. . . .

From Chapter 2 of *Matthew Arnold*, Longmans, London, New York, Toronto, 1955, pp. 75–81.

MURRAY KRIEGER

# *Dover Beach* and the Tragic
# Sense of Eternal Recurrence

What are the characteristics of Matthew Arnold's 'Dover Beach' that
have earned a place for the poem so far above that of those maligned
Victorian works which critics commonly consign to our wilful neglect?
To what extent has it earned its exemption from the common charges
they bring against many of its contemporaries?

It would seem clear enough that in 'Dover Beach' Arnold brings
along his usual equipment, or, I might better term it, his *impedimenta*.
The usual techniques and the usual patterns of thought which infect
much of his verse and render it unsuccessful are apparent at once. The
surprise is that the joining of them in this poem proves as happy as it
does. There is, first, the well-known Arnold melancholy: the man of
little faith in a world of no faith, who still hopes to maintain the spiritual
dignity which the world of no faith now seems to deny him. There is
also the typical nineteenth-century didactic formula which Arnold
rarely failed to use by allowing his 'poetic' observer to extort symbolic
instruction from a natural scene. Finally there is here as elsewhere the
mixture, perhaps the strange confusion, between a poetic diction and a
diction that is modern, almost prosaic.

Arnold's easy but uneven rhetoric of melancholy often leads these
characteristics to fail as he compounds them, but here they succeed,
and in a way that reaches beyond the limitations of Arnold's period and
of his own poetic sensibility. 'Dover Beach' bears and rewards contemplation from the vantage point of the modern, and yet ancient,
concept of time which has stirred our consciousness through writers like
Mann, Proust, Virginia Woolf, T. S. Eliot—a concept of time as exis-
tential rather than as chronologically historical, as the flow of Bergson's
dynamics, as the eternal and yet never-existing present. This awareness
which we associate with our sophisticated contemporary can be seen
somehow to emerge from Arnold's highly Victorian 'Dover Beach'. We
must determine how it manages to do so, how the very weaknesses that
generally characterize Arnold's poetic imagination serve here to create
this tragic and extremely modern vision. It is a vision which Arnold
achieves neither as a nineteenth-century optimist nor as a vague and
confused rebel of his period who turns to an equally nineteenth-century
pessimism and simple melancholy; it is a vision which he achieves by

transcending his period and foreseeing the intellectual crisis which we too often think of as peculiar to our own century.[1]

A cursory reading of the poem discloses that all the stanzas but the second are built on a similar two-part structure and that each recalls the ones which have gone before. The first section in each of these stanzas deals with that which is promising, hopeful; the second undercuts the cheer allowed by the first section and replaces the illusory optimism with a reality which is indeed barren, hopeless. In these subdivisions of stanzas there is also a sharp contrast in tone between the pleasant connotations of the first section of these stanzas and the less happy ones of the second. In each of them too, there is a contrast between the appeal to the sense of sight in the first section and the appeal to the sense of hearing in the second.

And yet, these three stanzas are not, of course, mere repetitions of each other. Each marks a subsequent development of the image—the conflict between the sea and the land. With each succeeding stanza the sea takes on a further meaning. I said earlier that this, like most of Arnold's poems, deals with a natural scene and the moral application of the meaning perceived within it: the vehicle of the metaphor and then the tenor carefully stated for us. In this poem, however, the development from the natural scene to the human levels into which it opens is much more successfully handled than elsewhere in his work. Each level grows into the succeeding one without losing the basic natural ingredients which initiated the image.

We can see that the natural scene described in the first stanza is value-laden from the beginning. It is clear that nature itself—or at least nature as sensuously perceived—does have immediate significance, and moral significance, so that when the development and application are made later, we do not feel them as unnatural. By the third stanza the sea has of course become the 'Sea of Faith',[2] but the human relevance of the sea-land imagery is justified by the transitional second stanza. In addition, the image is handled completely in the terms which characterize its natural use in the first stanza. The sea-land conflict is still with us, still the motivating force of the insight the poem offers. And in the last stanza the sea-land conflict exists in the present, but, for Arnold and for these lovers, representative here of humanity at large,

---

[1] This paragraph may seem to imply that Nietzsche, whose phrase I have borrowed for my title and my theme, is a twentieth-century mind. In the sense in which Arnold is predominantly a nineteenth-century mind, Nietzsche may very well appear rather to belong in our own century.

[2] The surface triteness of this phrase is typical of Arnold's frequent and stereotyped use of a metaphorical sea, as in the many variations on 'the Sea of Life' which dot his poems. (See, for example, 'To Marguerite', 'Despondency,' 'Human Life', 'Self-Dependence', 'A Summer Night', and 'The Buried Life'). His failure to exploit this image freshly or even to show an awareness of the need for doing so accounts in large part for his poetic weaknesses elsewhere. We shall see later that 'Dover Beach' is distinguished by Arnold's ability here to make his usual conception come alive through his manipulation of the central image of the poem.

D

the historical present. The aphoristic impressiveness of the final lines of the poem is again justified in terms of the initial image of the first stanza, which they here recall and bring to its final fruition. The archetypal image of the sea, of the tides, and of the action of these as the sea meets the land—all these have been merged with the destiny of that humanity to which they have meant so much throughout its mythopoetic history.

As nature has thus—if I may use the word—*naturally* merged with man, so, through the use of the middle part of the poem, has history merged with the present, has the recurrence, of which the sea, the tides, the meeting of land and sea have always stood as symbols, merged with the ever-historical present. This is why the second stanza of the poem is excluded from the parallel development of the others. It is the stanza which makes the poem possible, which brings us to 'the ebb and flow of *human* misery', and brings us to the past even as we remain in the present. The image and its archetypal quality are indispensable to the poem. For the tidal ebb and flow, retreat and advance, and the endless nature of these are precisely what is needed to give Arnold the sense of the eternal recurrence which characterizes the full meaning of the poem.

But now to examine some of these general comments in greater detail by looking at the poem more closely. The first eight lines give us the scene as it appeals immediately to the sight of the poet viewing it. It is a good scene, one which finds favour with the poet. The value of the scene is indicated by adjectives like 'calm', 'full', 'fair', 'tranquil', 'sweet', 'moon-blanched'. There is a sense of satisfaction, of utter completeness about the scene. But of course it is the sea which gives the feeling of ultimate pleasure. In the two places in which the land is mentioned there is something a bit less steady in the impression. The light on the French coast is not, after all, a steady light, and as it gleams and is gone so the cliffs of England, which seem to stand so steadily, yet are glimmering even as they are vast. The land, then, provides the only inconstancy, indeed the only qualification of the perfection of the scene.

The word 'only' in line 7 introduces the contrasting mood which will characterize the later portion of the stanza. But before this later portion is given to us, there is the remainder of line 7 and all of line 8, which serve as a reminder of the satisfying first portion of the stanza, although 'only' has already been introduced as a transition—one which serves to awaken us to the more unhappy attitude that is to follow. And with the word 'listen' at the beginning of line 9, we are to be shocked out of our happy lethargy even as the poet is shocked out of his. The sharp trochaic foot and the long caesura which follows re-enforce this emphasis. And with this word we are transferred from the visual world to the auditory world.

One might almost say that the poet, until this point remarking about the perfection of the scene, has been remarking rather casually—that is, after an almost random glance at it. But here he meets the scene more intimately. He does not merely glance but comes into closer rapport with the scene by lending the more contiguous sense, that of his hearing. He now pays close attention to the scene, and what he hears replaces what he has merely seen as a casual onlooker. What he discovers is far less satisfying, and yet it is more profound than his earlier reaction because he now begins to catch the undertones and overtones of the scene before him, which he before was content to witness superficially. And here the sea is used much as, for example, Conrad and Melville use it. Its superficial placidity, which beguiles its viewer, belies the perturbed nature, the 'underground' quality, of its hidden depths. As the more intimate, more aware, and more concerned faculty of hearing is introduced, the turmoil of sea meeting land becomes sensible. The shift in tone from the earlier portion of the stanza is made obvious by Arnold's use of 'grating roar' immediately after the appeal to the ear has been made.

One may see in the shift from the eye to the ear also another purpose. It is Arnold's way of moving us from the here and the now to the everywhere and always, from the specific immediacy of the present scene to the more universal application his image must have to serve the rest of the poem. What we *see* must be a particular scene which is unique and irreplaceable, while our hearing may be lulled by similarities to identify the sounds of other places and other times with those before us now.[3] No sight is completely like any other; sounds may be far more reminiscent and may thus allow us to fancy that we are in another time, in another country. Identity of sound may lead the imagination to an identity of occasion.[4] Then not only is the sense of sight inadequate to grasp the profound perplexities of the situation so that the more subtle sense of hearing must be invoked, but, unlike the sense of hearing, the sense of sight is also incapable of permitting us to break free of the relentless clutch of the present occasion to wander relaxedly up and down the immensities of time.

The 'eternal note of sadness', then, caused by the endless battle without victory and without truce between sea and land; this note representing the give-and-take of the tide which symbolically echoes the basic rhythmic pattern of human physio-psychology—this eternal note of sadness, heard also by Sophocles, connects the past at once with the presentness of the past and connects also this rhythmic pattern with the humanity who has taught it to serve them and yet ironically, as

[3] I am indebted to Michael W. Dunn, who first suggested to me that Arnold is here using the greater dependence of the sense of sight on a single time-and-place occurrence.

[4] One can see a similar conceit operating in Wordsworth's 'To the Cuckoo' and Keats' 'Ode to a Nightingale'. In each of these works, too, the poet (who here cannot use his sense of sight since he is unable to see the bird) allows himself to fancy, because only the sound of the bird's song reaches his senses, that the bird itself is somehow immortal even while it has temporal existence, that it has sung in other times and in other places. The illusion fostered by this romantic operation of synecdoche could become a valuable poetic instrument in the hands of such writers as these.

the Greeks among others have shown us, has instead served it. Even in the first stanza we saw nature as animated by the human mind, as immediately meaningful in human terms. In the second stanza its human relevance is made explicit. The word 'turbid' (line 17) effectively joins the natural sense of the image to its human application as it combines the meaning of 'muddied' with that of 'confused'. As Sophocles serves to read man into the natural image of the first stanza, thus making him one with the natural world, so with the final word ('we') of line 18 the present is read into the past;[5] and the circle of the natural order, now including within its circumference the wheel of human destiny and man-made time, is closed.

The third stanza, in a manner parallel to the first, breaks into two contrasting parts. The first three lines present the promise of the visual image, the last five the despair of the auditory. In the first portion, to the sense of fullness and perfection which was ours in the first lines of the poem is now added the illusion of protectiveness—hence the 'girdle' image. Not only is the sea characterized by its complete and self-sufficient perfection, but, like the divine 'One' of Plotinus, it must over-flow its bounds to salve, indeed to anoint, the imperfect land. Thanks to the passage on Sophocles, the extension of the sea to the human problem and hence to the 'Sea of Faith' is now literally as well as metaphorically justified, although the image must remain true to its earlier formulation. And it does. After the 'but' (line 24), which here has the same qualifying function as the disappointed 'only' in the first stanza, we are returned to the sense of hearing and to the struggle between land and sea which it first introduced. The inevitable cycle must continue and every resurgence be followed by the equally neces-sary retreat. The advance we have made from the sea to the sea of faith and the added quality of protectiveness given by the 'girdle' image bestow a new dimension to the hopelessness of the 'naked shingles of the world', the words which close the stanza.

While the first line and a half of the last stanza, in which the poet addresses his beloved, may seem digressive, although they are prepared for in line 6 of the first stanza, they are involved in the development of the poem by the crucial adjective 'true,' which here means 'faithful': the poet is posing the only and the hardly satisfying alternative—the personal alternative of mutual fidelity—for our abandonment by the sea of faith. And again there follows the antithesis between the vision which yields the Apollonian attitude and the cacophony of Dionysian turmoil. Here, however, the balance is swung more heavily than before in the direction of despair, For, we are told explicitly, the world of perfection now merely 'seems' (line 30); the world of chaos exists

---

[5] The effecting of this union may be aided by what may seem to be something like an unusual internal rhyme between two neighbouring vowels, between the last syllable of 'misery' and 'we'. (It would of course be difficult to maintain this as an internal rhyme if one admits that the last syllable of 'misery' is probably unstressed.)

'really' (line 33). The final image of battle, though far-grown from the land-sea conflict of the latter lines of the first stanza, is thoroughly consistent with it and can take its meaning only in terms of it. We are returned in effect to the pre-human natural world of the first stanza and to its primitivism as the clashing armies are finally characterized by the poet as 'ignorant'. The clash is endless, as endless as time and tide, and, viewed without faith, in terms of nothingness, is as purposeless. Man himself has now drawn his circle closed or rather has acknowledged the closedness of nature's circle—perhaps the same thing—and has joined with an undergrounded nature to assert his ignorance, his irresponsibility, his doom. But the doom man carries with him he carries only to assert with it his eternal recurrence, even if that which recurs does so but to be doomed again. For paradoxically, doom too is eternally recurrent.

We are, then, worse than returned to what I called a moment ago the pre-human natural world of the first stanza and its primitivism. For the 'nature' of the first stanza, being, as we have seen, value-laden, existing only in terms of human perception, was indeed a nature that was humanized. It was seen as meaningful, indeed as purposive. The telic quality of the human was read into nature and, by animating it, made it also telic. But in the primitivism of the *'ignorant* armies' humanity is seen as atelic. The relationship has been reversed as the non-purposive quality of the nature of modern science has been read into man. As nature was humanized at the start, so here man is naturalized and, thus, deprived of his purposiveness, deadened. He has indeed become part of nature and hence, in the words of Keats, 'become a sod'. The poet, of course, rises above this death-in-life by his dedication to the personal, the I-and-Thou, relationship to his beloved, now that any more inclusive relationships have been shut off from him. But, more important, the poet's assertion of his still-lingering humanity consists primarily in his insistence on realizing fully the sense of its loss, in his refusal to be 'ignorant' of it.

The poem may seem at first, despite some sideroads, to have a uni-linear chronological development. After the natural scene of the present is given us in the first stanza, the word 'eternal' in the last line of this stanza permits the poet to move back to Sophocles. Then, after briefly returning to the present in the latter part of the second stanza, the poet moves us back again in time, but now to the Christian Middle Ages.[6] With the introduction of the modern world and its scepticism in the latter part of the third stanza, the poet has prepared us to return to the present dramatic scene of the last stanza. But whatever sense of chronology this arrangement allows us is seen to be purely illusory because of

[6] Here we see Arnold managing to return to one of the favourite laments of so much of his prose as well as his verse: the irreplaceable psychological efficacy of the Christian medieval unity which, unfortunately, had to turn out to be so scientifically erroneous, and thus to him unacceptable, in its theological foundations.

the return in the final image of the poem to the primitivism and everlastingness of the image of tidal conflict with which we began. Similarly, in the very close parallelism of structure of the first, third, and concluding stanzas we feel the unprogressiveness of man's ever-repetitive circular history.

The handling of the metrics and rhyme scheme reflect the other elements we have observed in the poem. The inexorable quality of the unending struggle as it is felt in such passages as

. . . the grating roar
Of pebbles which the waves draw back, and fling,
At their return, up the high strand,
Begin, and cease, and then again begin . . .

is obvious enough. But perhaps more significant is the development of the patterns of line-length and rhyme, which begin as relatively un-defined and conclude as firm and under full control. Through the first three stanzas the intermixture of pentameter lines with shorter ones is unpredictable, and, similarly, there is no determinate rhyme scheme. While the poem clearly is written in rhyme, the echoes of the final syllables of the lines surprise us since there is no pattern which enables us to foresee when the sounds will recur. And yet they continually do recur in this seemingly undetermined way. Only the final word of line 9 ('roar') seems not to have any rhyme in its stanza; and even this may be claimed to be an off-rhyme with 'fair' (line 2) and 'air' (line 6), functioning to set up a tension between this line and the earlier pleasant portion of the stanza—precisely what we should expect of the noun which is characterized as 'grating'.

Thus until the last stanza is reached, the patternless rhymes suggest a continual recurrence, but one on which human meaning and form have not yet been bestowed. The echoes multiply, but they have not yet been cast into a significant mould. In the final stanza a clear rhyme scheme at last emerges (*abbacddcc*), and, further, for the first time the line-lengths even out. Between the initial trimeter and the concluding tetrameter are seven consistently pentameter lines. The problem of the poem, while certainly not resolved (poems rarely resolve problems, or ought to), has at last emerged as fully comprehensible, in terms of the poem at least. The meaning of the recurrence has become tragically and profoundly clear.

It may—and perhaps with some justice—be claimed that, if my prosodic analysis is valid, this manipulation of line-length and rhyme is, after all, a not very cunning trick, indeed is a highly mechanical contrivance. Or the poet's attempt to make the technical elements so obviously expressive may be charged and booked under Yvor Winters' 'fallacy of imitative form'. I shall skirt these issues since my purpose here is primarily explicative. In terms of this purpose it is enough to say that the versification, like the structure, the diction, and the archetypal imagery, marks out the repetitive inclusiveness of the human condition and its purposeless gyrations. The poem's form thus comes to be a commentary on the problem that is being poetically explored, a mirror which allows the poem to come to terms with itself.

But if the form helps indicate the price of eternal recurrence for a world robbed of its faith—the fate of being pitilessly bound by the inescapable circle—in the regularity it finally achieves, it indicates, too, the sole possibility for victory over the circle and freedom from it: the more than natural, the felt human awareness of its existence and its meaning. The tragic is at least an attainment, an attainment through the painful process of utter realization, realization of self, of nature, and of history. And the contemporaneity of the Western tradition in the poem is Arnold's way of proving that he has realized *it* and himself as its child.

From *The Play and Place of Criticism*, The Johns Hopkins Press, Baltimore, 1967, pp. 69–77.

HOWARD W. FULWEILER

# *The Forsaken Merman*

. . . Arnold's sources for 'The Forsaken Merman' and his changes from
them do much to reveal his approach to the story. Tinker and Lowry
suggest that Arnold may have used either George Borrow's translation
of the Danish ballad, 'The Deceived Merman', or his prose account of
the story in a review of Just Mathias Thiele's *Danske Folkesagn*.[1] In
the Danish originals the point of view is that of the land-dwelling human
beings as opposed to the non-human inhabitants of the sea. The story
is not about a merman; it is about a human being, Grethe or Agnes, as
she is variously called; it shows little sympathy for the merman or his
children. At the conclusion of the prose account we are told that 'Grethe
ever after stayed with her parents, and let the merman himself take care
of his ugly little children'; in Borrow's translation of the ballad, the
merman (who is described as a fair demon with yellow eyes and a green
beard) begs the girl to consider the children:

> Think on them, Agnes, think on them all;
> Think on the great one, think on the small.

Her answer to her unnatural lover is calmly unsympathetic:

> Little, O little care I for them all,
> Or for the great one, or for the small.

As in so much poetry of the Victorian age, the age of the dramatic
monologue, point of view in 'The Forsaken Merman' is revealing. In
opposition to his immediate sources and to many of the less immediate
analogues in the myths of Beauty and the Beast and Cupid and Psyche,
Arnold has shifted the sympathies of the reader from his fellow human
being to an alien creature—from the familiar beauty to the unknown
beast. The shift in point of view accomplishes two things: first, it
increases our sympathy with the pathos of the merman's hopeless plight;
second, it increases the guilt associated with Margaret's faithlessness.
Later on I shall try to suggest some reasons for Arnold's shift in
emphasis.

The most powerful expression of Arnold's reversal of the values of
his sources is not found in point of view, however, but in the careful
precision of the imagery he uses to develop the fundamental land-sea
conflict in the poem. Arnold creates a sharp contrast between the

---

[1] *Commentary on the Poetry of Matthew Arnold*, Oxford University Press, 1940,
pp. 130–2.

merman's free and colourful water-world and Margaret's walled and achromatous village. He distinguishes the red gold throne in the heart of the sea vividly from the 'white-wall'd town, / And the little grey church on the windy shore'. He sets the freedom of the sea folk and their 'wild white horses' in the boundless infinities of the ocean against the walls around the village, the 'narrow paved streets' within the walls, and the 'small leaded panes' of the church. The merman and his children must look through the narrow windows to see Margaret sitting close to the pillar because 'shut stands the door'. In order to see through the windows, they must stand on grave stones. Similarly, the emotional satisfactions of the sea are indicated in the abandoned children and in the more direct eroticism of the coiling and twining sea-snakes in opposition to the chilly sexlessness of the town where even the mother and father of Arnold's sources are replaced by a reference to kinsfolk praying in the church.[2] Despite the erotic and aesthetic freedom of the sea in comparison to the land, Arnold does not, as one might suspect, find the moral aspects of the land superior to those of the sea. Although Margaret sat on a red gold throne, 'the youngest sate on her knee', and 'She comb'd its bright hair, and she tended it well'. Yet when the merman calls and the 'little ones moan' outside the church, Margaret refuses to answer them:

> But, ah, she gave me never a look,
> For her eyes were seal'd to the holy book!
> Loud prays the priest; shut stands the door.  (ll. 80–83)

Perhaps the most striking contrast is the peaceful tranquility of life in the sea as opposed to the ceaseless activity of the land. The merman and his family dwell in

> Sand-strewn caverns, cool and deep,
> Where the winds are all asleep;
> Where the spent lights quiver and gleam.  (ll. 35–37)

They are able to live secure from the world in an abode of meditative silence; they have achieved that state which Arnold later called 'disinterestedness' not by being above the fitful tempests of practical life, but by being below them. Life in the town, however, is characterized by constant movement—if not 'sick hurry'. Arnold's skilful employment of present participles increases the effect of incessant and mechanical activity. The town is 'humming', the spinning wheel is 'whizzing', Margaret is 'singing',

> For the humming street, and the child with its toy!
> For the priest, and the bell, and the holy well,
> For the wheel where I spun,
> And the blessed light of the sun!  (ll. 90–93)

[2] It is interesting to speculate on how much of Arnold's imagery in 'The Forsaken Merman' was suggested by two early and highly erotic poems of Tennyson, 'The Mermaid' and 'The Merman'. The similarity was noted by the reviewer of the 1849 volume for *Fraser's Magazine*, Vol. 39, May 1849, p. 576.

Even the need for prayer, which had originally brought about Margaret's return from the depths, is represented as a mechanical and formalized 'murmur of folk at their prayers'. Arnold's opposition of sea and land suggests more, however, than a Tennysonian dichotomy between action and inaction as in 'The Lotos-Eaters' or even an Arnoldian dialectic of disinterestedness opposed to the philistine world of 'practice'. The depths are not only a peaceful retreat; they reveal the fundamental mysteries of the universe. For 'ranged all round' the deep caverns are those primal forces of nature, the sea-beasts and sea-snakes, already identified by Tennyson in 'The Mermaid' and 'The Kraken' with the final mysteries of sex, life and death. Here the sea people witness a reality undreamed of by the surface-bound townsfolk as the 'great whales come sailing by', their all-seeing eyes open in their eternal circumnavigation of the world. The cool, dark caverns of the merman assume, then, the profoundly revelatory function of the underground or undersea experience characteristic of myths and dreams. In the town there is a monotonous and colourless whirring, whizzing, humming, murmuring and praying behind walls and shut doors, and among grave stones. In the sea there is colour, imagination, life, love, and the hidden and mysterious meaning of the world.

But what, we may now ask, does all of this mean? The answer is a complex one, but worth, I think, considerable effort in obtaining. Johnson has read the conflict between the sea and the 'human land' as 'associated . . . with the conflict between the isolated natural self and the social or moral self'.[3] Arnold, in this interpretation, has used Easter, the time of resurrection, to add meaning to Margaret's rising from the 'grave-like, womb-like caverns of the sea' and her return from 'natural to human life'. Her triumph over nature, however, results in necessary pain and suffering. 'If she has gained her soul, which she was in danger of losing with the merman, she has lost her love, her natural delights: in a certain sense she has had to lose her life in order to find it. This is Easter from the point of view of the depths'.[4]

The chief difficulty with this interpretation, it seems to me, is that this is not 'Easter from the point of view of the depths'; it is Easter from the point of view of Margaret. It assumes that the story is more about Margaret than it is about the merman. Yet it is clear that Arnold manipulated his sources to place his chief emphasis on the merman. Although Johnson suggests that 'Arnold does imaginatively join the two, even as he reveals them in conflict', the theme of the poem in this reading still contrasts 'the way of the animal' to the 'moral way'.[5]

Arnold's imagery, however, seems to show us something quite different from a simple conflict between natural instincts and human or religious moral standards. Arnold's subtle shift in point of view from

    [3] W. Stacy Johnson, *The Voices of Matthew Arnold: An Essay in Criticism*, New Haven, 1961, p. 84.
    [4] *The Voices of Matthew Arnold*, p. 87.
    [5] *The Voices of Matthew Arnold*, p. 89.

his sources and his carefully controlled development of imagery create, instead of a simple conflict between erotic love and moral duty, a poem complex in meaning and profoundly ironic. Superficially Arnold takes what is traditionally amoral, alien, and treacherous (a merman) and contrasts him to what is traditionally moral, familiar, and faithful (the everyday life of conventionally religious human beings in a small town). In fact, however, the qualities of each are reversed. The sea, in Arnold's poem, represents freedom, beauty, love, and the deepest mysteries of life, yet paradoxically it also represents moral responsibility to others, as in the care of children. The land represents imprisonment by convention, insensitivity to the deepest moral values, and monotonous, mechanical, incessant activity. Margaret's failure to respond to the mysterious beauty of the sea, 'the sea of faith' as Arnold was significantly to call it in 'Dover Beach', does *not* result in her losing her life to gain it; instead, it chronicles her tragic refusal to give herself completely to the depths. For Margaret, Easter is not a symbolic resurrection from death to life; it is, as she implies to the merman, only a legal observance to save herself. Easter symbolizes Margaret's ironic failure to accept real life. She is reborn, not into life, but into spiritual death. Moreover, through exquisite irony Arnold shows that her choice of conventional morality and her timorous rejection of the depths of being cause her to commit the most shocking immorality, the Judas sin—treachery. . . .

From 'Matthew Arnold: The Metamorphosis of a Merman', *Victorian Poetry*, Vol. I, 1963, pp. 208-22 (208-12).

A. E. DYSON

# The Scholar-Gipsy

'The Scholar-Gipsy' is undoubtedly a finer poem than Dr Leavis's assessment in *The Common Pursuit* (p. 30) suggests. The phrases used there are 'weak confusion' and 'intellectual debility'—and one must suggest, with due deference to an often perceptive critic, that these will not do at all. There is, then, cause to be grateful to Professor G. Wilson Knight for taking the poem seriously, and performing an analysis both careful and illuminating (*Review of English Studies*, N.S. Vol. 6, 1955, pp. 53–62).

When this debt is acknowledged, however, it must be added that Mr Wilson Knight's interpretation is too subjective to pass without a challenge, especially in so far as he commits himself to a theory that the wisdom of a poem is not necessarily the same as the wisdom of its poet. This theory allows Mr Wilson Knight to attach to the poem his own wisdom, but only at the expense of ignoring what seem most likely to have been Arnold's intentions.

Mr Wilson Knight points to the importance of oriental references in the two concluding stanzas of the poem, and tells us that 'we must accordingly search within the main body of the poem for qualities roughly corresponding to the oriental powers symbolized by the Tyrian trader'. Such 'qualities' he finds in the scholar gipsy himself, and on the strength of them is soon identifying the gipsy with Dionysian powers (as against the Apollonian Oxford of the poem), and with intuitive wisdom (as against the cold touch of analytical intellect). The gipsy has an essentially undergraduate wisdom, an 'eternal immaturity'—and this distinguishes him from the dons, whose greater knowledge has made it hard for them to retain 'wisdom'. The gipsy exemplifies 'the essence of true learning; the opening of the mind, the wonder, the intuition of fields unexplored. That is why the presiding deity of a great university [and he is no less than this] may be felt as the eternal undergraduate.' The dons are lacking in his qualities, and need his energy and freshness to preserve them from complete desiccation. These dons are symbolized by the 'One' on the 'Intellectual throne', in whom 'the essentially backward, devitalized, "realistic", thinking of the contemporary intellect is personified. The state indicated is unhealthy, nerveless, and guilty of self-pity.'

Now this is, admittedly, a possible point of view, and one from which a poem similar to 'The Scholar-Gipsy' could have been written. Had Blake, or Carlyle, or D. H. Lawrence had the handling of the material, it would no doubt have come out in this sort of way. But one wonders what the author of *Literature and Dogma* and *God and the Bible* would have had to comment on such a point of view, and whether he would not have regarded the One on the 'intellectual throne' as being superior to the gipsy in insight and integrity, even though less well placed than the gipsy for the enjoyment of an 'eternal week-end' (Dr Leavis's phrase). My contention here will be that Arnold never commits himself to the gipsy (as both Dr Leavis and Mr Wilson Knight assume), but that he is aware of him all the time as the embodiment of an illusion. This is the reason why 'The Scholar-Gipsy' has a greater strength than Dr Leavis allows, and a greater centrality to the thought of its creator than is indicated by Mr Wilson Knight.

'Arnold's poem', says Mr Wilson Knight, 'confronts our western tradition with suggestions of a wisdom, lore, or magic of oriental affinities or origin.' And having said this, he assumes that the confrontation is almost entirely to the detriment of the western tradition—thereby stating his own view, but ignoring that which we know to have been Arnold's. He speaks also of 'the poem's total meaning, which strives, as its title "The Scholar-Gipsy" as good as tells us, towards a fusion of two traditions, western and eastern'. But for my own part, I fail to see how the title 'as good as tells us' any such thing, unless we are predisposed to read it in this way: and in view of Mr Wilson Knight's admission that Arnold himself might have been unaware of his poem's wisdom, it is hard to see how it could.

It might be truer to suggest that 'The Scholar-Gipsy' confronts the joyful illusions of an earlier age with the melancholy realism of the nineteenth century, and that in this confrontation, with its complex emotional tensions, the really moving quality of the poem is to be found. Arnold was as aware of the difficulties of 'belief' as any Victorian, and as determined as George Eliot to live and think 'without opium'. Like the majority of his contemporaries, though somewhat ahead of most of them, he had heard the 'sea of faith' retreating with its 'melancholy, long, withdrawing roar'. In *God and the Bible* he does not hesitate to analogize the gospel miracles to the tale of Cinderella—pleasing, emotionally comforting, but unhappily not *true*. And because they are not true, there can be no question of our continuing to believe them merely for our own comfort.

> The more we may have been helped to be faithful, humble and charitable by taking the truth of this story, and other stories equally legendary, for granted, the greater is our embarrassment, no doubt, at having to do without them  But we have to do without them none the less on that account.

Arnold shared with many seventeenth- and eighteenth-century thinkers a disbelief in Christian and medieval thought forms, but he did not share with them an easy contempt for everything that man had believed outside the context of 'Right Reason' and scientific empiricism.

On the contrary, he recognized in the earlier culture a beauty, a joy, an emotional and moral value, that could be envied by his own perplexed and troubled age: envied, but not regained. The fact seemed to be (and 'fact', 'belief', 'truth' were much simpler concepts to the Victorians, we must remember, than they are often thought to be today) that these earlier ages were happier than the nineteenth century, but that they were also inaccessible to it; that they were capable of sustaining man in a more joyful and serene existence, but only at the cost of a certain 'want of intellectual seriousness' (nourished upon intellectual ignorance) that was no longer acceptable. The opening lines of an early poem by Yeats capture that wistful and 'High Serious' acceptance of disenchantment which is so characteristically Victorian:

> The woods of Arcady are dead
>   And over is their antique joy,
> Of old the world on dreaming fed,
>   Grey truth is now her painted toy.

Arnold, however, though regretting his losses, was a realist, and a prophet of the future. Behind his thought in 'The Scholar-Gipsy' there was, I fancy, a *Weltanschauung* not dissimilar to that of Comte. He saw the world as an evolving organism which, like a human being, had progressed through childhood and youth to maturity. The earlier 'explanations' of things, theological and metaphysical, had been those appropriate to immaturity—glad, carefree, invigorating, but not grounded in reality.[1] When the world at last came of age, it had had to put away childish things. And even if the long-awaited maturity did sometimes resemble a premature old age, with the Victorian *avant-garde* haggard under the burden of its own enlightenment, there was nothing that could be done to mend the situation. Can a man enter the second time into his mother's womb and be born? In 'The Scholar-Gipsy' Arnold's attitude to the gipsy is closely analogous to that of an adult towards a child. He appreciates and even envies its innocence, but realizes that no return to such a state is possible for himself. The child loses its 'innocence' not by some act of sin, nor by a defect of intellect, but merely by gaining experience and developing into an adult. The realities of adult life turn out to be less agreeable, in many respects, than childish fantasies, but there can be no question of thinking them less true.

The gipsy, like a child, is the embodiment of a good lost, not of a good temporarily or culpably mislaid. When Arnold contrasts the gipsy's serenity with the disquiets and perplexities of his own age, he is not satirizing the nineteenth century, or renouncing it, or criticizing it, or

---

[1] 'Our religion, parading evidences such as those on which the popular mind relies now; our philosophy, pluming itself on its reasonings about causation and finite and infinite being; what are they but the shadows and dreams and false shows of knowledge? The day will come when we shall wonder at ourselves for having trusted to them, for having taken them seriously' ('The Study of Poetry', *Essays in Criticism, Second Series*).

suggesting a remedy. He is, rather, exploring its spiritual and emotional losses, and the stoic readjustment which these will entail for it.

Dr Leavis has written as though Arnold laid his head to sleep, and gave his heart a holiday. But Arnold's stoic acceptance of unpalatable realities is among the most impressive qualities of his best poems, and 'escapism' is not a charge we should bring against them. There is no need to insist upon the naked dignity of such statements as this:

> The world which seems
> To lie before us as a land of dreams,
> So various, so beautiful, so new
> Hath really neither joy, nor love, nor light,
> Nor certitude, nor peace, nor help for pain . . .

or as this:

> Not as their friend or child I speak!
> But as on some far northern strand,
> Thinking of his own gods, a Greek
> In pity and mournful awe might stand
> Before some fallen runic stone—
> For both were faiths, and both are gone. . . .

The diction and tone are their own best evidence of costly intellectual integrity. In his prose, Arnold tried hard to salvage from the Christian wreckage an 'Eternal-not-ourselves-that-makes-for-righteousness'. But in his poetry there is a sterner discipline of self-knowledge, and the full extent of the Victorian predicament—a tragic predicament for men of Arnold's temperament—is embodied.

It was not for nothing that Arnold laid stress upon the gipsy's magic art. At the Renaissance (if an old-fashioned use of this word can be allowed) man set out on a search for temporal power. Bacon, the prophet of the movement, looks forward not only to Newton and Locke, but also to the Industrial Revolution, and to the Victorian idea of 'progress'. In the sixteenth century, science and magic were the two principal techniques for gaining power. By the nineteenth century science had vindicated its material usefulness with results, magic had failed to produce results and been discredited. Science, however, had proved to have a sting in its tail, since the spiritual losses entailed by the acceptance of empiricism as a total account of reality were becoming yearly more apparent. Magic, on the other hand, could still, in fantasy, be thought of as an ideal and unqualified means of power, even though it were now known not to work. Science had become an enemy of religion and enchantment, the discoverer of a universe of death: magic could still be identified with dreams of a richer life in a more satisfactory universe, since its very failure liberated it for poetic use as

> an abstraction,
> Remaining a perpetual possibility
> Only in a world of speculation.[2]

[2] Borrowed from Mr Eliot's *Burnt Norton*.

The scholar gipsy embodies, then, the optimistic but chimerical hopes of an earlier age. He waits for 'the spark from Heaven to fall' (st. 12), but he waits in vain: the spark does not fall, as the nineteenth century has discovered for itself (st. 18–20). This realization is in the rhythms and tone of the poem which is reflective and melancholy in the elegiac mode, not filled with dynamic hope. The gipsy is committed to a discredited art, and so exiled from Oxford. In st. 8, as he looks down on the lighted city at night, he looks not as a presiding deity but as a long superseded ghost from the past. His very nature forbids him to enter, since one touch of Victorian realism would reveal him for the wraith he is (st. 23). The situation is not unlike that of the young Jude gazing eagerly towards the lights of that same city—not to Oxford itself, however, but to the ideal city which his childish dreams have superimposed. The scholar gipsy turns away from the real Oxford, and seeks his 'straw' in 'Some sequester'd grange'. His place is with the primitive, the uncultured, the unintellectual. Only so can he survive at all, so late in history.

In *Literature and Dogma* and *God and the Bible* Arnold insists that he is writing not for those who are still happy with their Christian illusions (the Victorian version of 'simple faith'), but only for those highly serious few who still value the illusions whilst being unable honestly to accept them. The scholar gipsy would not have been one of the readers Arnold had in mind: he would have been one of the happier (though perhaps less honest) band who enjoyed the faith of earlier ages simply because they had not been intellectually awakened to reality in Oxford. The gipsy is essentially outside Oxford; and his exclusion, though it tells against the happiness of Oxford, tells even more against the acceptability of the gipsy.

A similar balance will be found in Arnold's well-known prose passage about Oxford. He expresses his love of the idealized city, 'steeped in sentiment as she lies, spreading her gardens to the moon-light, and whispering from her towers the last enchantments of the Middle Ages . . . unravaged by the fierce intellectual life of our century'. But this Oxford is a moonlit vision, a dream woven of those 'last enchantments' which Arnold was doing as much as anyone to dispel. For Arnold was not himself unravaged by the fierce intellectual life of his century, nor did he expect the other inhabitants of Oxford to be. His moonlit Oxford, like the scholar gipsy, may still be as beautiful as a dream and calling us to the ideal: but can an honest man build his life on dreams? The home of 'lost causes, and forsaken beliefs, and un-popular names, and impossible loyalties' remains an ideal to preserve us from becoming Philistines: but the causes are lost, and the beliefs forsaken; the names unpopular and the loyalties impossible.[3] In this

---

[3] Compare, for a similar complex of responses, Arnold's words about New-man in the introduction to his American discourse on Emerson, 1883: 'Oxford has more criticism now, more knowledge, more light; but such voices as those of our youth it has no longer. The name of Cardinal Newman is a great name to the

Oxford, as in the idea of the scholar gipsy, the past tantalizes us with its beauty and its hopes: but we know that for all that the past is dead.

The Victorian predicament, insofar as Arnold represents it, was a tragic one—to desire with the heart what was rejected by the head, to need for the spirit what was excluded by the mind. But this is the tradition in which 'The Scholar-Gipsy' stands. The poem is not conceived, as Mr Wilson Knight would lead us to believe, in that parallel tradition of Romantic or Christian or Social solutions to the impasse.

## II

The first fourteen stanzas of the poem are on the whole the most memorable, and in these Arnold creates the myth of the gipsy. Analytical intellect is temporarily laid to sleep, but only in order that the myth may be evoked in its own strength to serve the organization of the poem as a whole. There is a dreamlike quality in the verse, in the direct tradition of Keats's 'Odes', and an elegaic note deriving from 'Il Penseroso' and Gray's 'Elegy'. In the 'Ode to a Nightingale' Keats wills his entry into an ideal world ('Away, away, for I will fly to thee'), and re-creates the song of the nightingale as a symbol of eternal beauty. But though the vision is a positive one, it still belongs to poetry, not to life. The word 'forlorn' recalls the poet to reality, to the world

Where beauty cannot keep her lustrous eyes,
Nor new love pine at them beyond tomorrow.

The nightingale of the vision can reveal the bitterness of life in time, but cannot provide an escape; it belongs to art, not to life. ('The fancy cannot cheat so well / As she is famed to do, deceiving elf.') The nightingale's song is vital and real as a symbol of what men desire, but has no reality beyond this. Similarly, Keats's Grecian urn has a life and vitality which, since it belongs to art, is more enduring than the experience of men in time: but this is attained only because it is not itself 'alive', and because it is not, outside the world of 'fancy', relevant to those who are. The happy lovers will never despair or fade, but neither will they kiss. The urn is a vision of fullness, but at the cost of being also 'Cold pastoral'.

The scholar gipsy is similar in his symbolic function to the nightingale's song and the Grecian urn. He is there to reveal the predicament of man's place in time, the ironic gulf between what man can dream of as possible and what he knows can possibly be. Arnold is no more confused between fact and fiction than Keats was, and to interpret the scholar gipsy as a 'programme' is the most basic mistake that can be made about the poem. The scholar gipsy's uselessness to the nineteenth

imagination still; his genius and his style are still things of power. But he is over eighty years of age; he is in the Oratory at Birmingham; he has adopted, for the doubts and difficulties which beset men's minds today, a solution which, to speak frankly, is impossible.'

century on a practical level is underlined, however, by his associations with magic and the pre-scientific world; and as I have suggested, the choice of such a central figure was not made by the poet in any arbitrary spirit.

The gipsy is never seen in the poem by cultured men, or by the dons; he is seen only by shepherds, children, maids dancing at night, simple men bathing on a summer day, the housewife at work, and other unsophisticated observers. It is the simplicity and 'faith' of these observers which enables them to see the gipsy; but the One on the intellectual throne does not see. (The non-readers of *Literature and Dogma*, we might say, see, but not the readers of that work.) The scholar gipsy has, then, the vividness and 'reality' of a child's vision—which is the reality of fancy working upon a consciousness alert and eager, but not the reality of anything apart from that. In st. 1, the evening atmosphere is numinous; in st. 2, the 'bleatings . . . distant cries' and so on are hypnotic, a summer evening's trance, relaxed and contented. In st. 3, the poet himself retires to a place apart, a bower sensuous and secluded where he can daydream. In st. 4, Arnold submits, like the gipsy, to an escape—but still in the mood of an afternoon's diversion. The gipsy escaped because he was 'tired of knocking at Preferment's door', tired of competition, and of the battle of life. He wanted to change his civilized society for a 'natural' or 'wild' one, to change intellect for intuition, the head for the heart. His desire was to roam freely outside the paths of convention, to achieve an integrated life apart from the blight of western culture.

He was, in fact, a primitivist, attempting to realize the myth of the noble savage: seeking eternal fulfilment in a world unoppressed by the pressure of civilization, and hoping that Time itself, man's enemy, could be cheated in this way.

But Arnold, of all men, knew a myth when he saw one. The Churchman who could equate Adam and Eve, and the Incarnation, with Cinderella, was not a man to be taken in by the Noble Savage, or to make such an elementary mistake about Time. His own ideal, as we know, was that of culture, and the scholar gipsy stands at the opposite pole to culture. The gipsy does not, we notice, have either the Hebraic or the Hellenic virtues as Arnold understood them. He does not combine sweetness with light, but on the contrary, 'does what he likes', and does so in ignorance of the Zeitgeist. He belongs, unmistakably, to innocence, not to experience; to the youth of the world, not to its maturity. He is a creature of superstition and credulity: a kindly creature, not a dark one, it is true, but when all is said, Arnold's own sympathies were with knowledge.

In st. 8 the gipsy is seen on 'retir'd ground'—withdrawn from experience, like the 'youth to fortune and to fame unknown' of Gray's 'Elegy'. Then he is seen in 'a pensive dream'. In st. 9 he is part of an enchanted spring evening, in st. 10 he is a midsummer vision. The suggestion of hypnosis is again irresistible, and in the sequence 'river

... bathing ... gone' there is more than the hint of a mirage. In st. 11
the uneducated housewife sees him, in st. 12 the animal world. But
through this sequence there is a subtle progression from Spring (st. 6),
to Summer (st. 8–10), to Autumn (st. 12). Finally, in st. 13, we arrive
at Winter, the season of deprivation and death. And it is here that
Arnold himself encounters the gipsy. His vision is the Oxford vision;
it is a vision of the gipsy battling through snow, rejected from the city,
in difficulties, turning away from the city. The gipsy must 'fly our
contact' for his safety. There can be no safety for *him* in a meeting with
the agnostic intellectual who envies him.

In st. 16 the gipsy is again considered in his symbolic role. When
contrasted with this symbol, the nineteenth-century losses are severe,
but they are beyond remedy—Time and the Zeitgeist are in alliance
against the gipsy. The opposite pole of the poem is the One on the
intellectual throne, and this is the pole, of course, at which Arnold
himself is. Romantics (including the Romantic within) may protest
against a devitalized cosmos, but the Highly Serious will be constrained
to accept. Despair, however, is not to be escaped, 'For none has hope
like thine': and patience, which is the stoic virtue demanded of the
disenchanted, is 'too close neighbour of despair'. In st. 20, therefore, the
final truth emerges, not explicitly, but in the suggestions of the imagery.
The reality of the scholar gipsy is *death*. He is in a place where there are
no more doubts and joy is unclouded, but such a place is only to be
equated with non-existence. In st. 14, Arnold has written

> Two hundred years are flown ...
> And thou from earth art gone
> Long since, and in some queit churchyard laid—

this being the stanza when he emerges from conscious daydreaming into
waking life, before returning to his myth for the second, contemporary
part of the poem. His recognition in this stanza of the gipsy's physical
death is recalled by the imagery of st. 20—though linked now with the
added, and deeper, suggestion of his death as a symbol also: 'And every
doubt long blown by time away....' 'Blown by time away' can suggest
only the dust of death—the death of a man ('Imperious Caesar, dead
and turned to clay / Might stop a hole to keep the wind away'), and the
death of an idea. Death is the gipsy's reality—for Arnold, at least, it is—
and that is why the poet meets him in Winter, and meets him as a
potential enemy.

And so the poem moves to its last major statement:

> But fly our paths, our feverish contact fly!
> For strong the infection of our mental strife,
>   Which, though it gives no bliss, yet spoils for rest;
> And we should win thee from thy own fair life,
>   Like us distracted, and like us unblest.
>     Soon, soon, thy cheer would die,

Thy hopes grow timorous, and unfix'd thy powers,
  And thy clear aims be cross and shifting made:
And then thy glad perennial youth would fade,
  Fade, and grow old at last, and die like ours.

Reading this, the last word before the closing simile, it seems clear
enough where Arnold himself, and the age he represented, stands. And
since the concreteness of the gipsy's symbolism is behind this stanza,
to give precision both to the ideas and to the emotions, the poem in its
totality realizes, complexly and poignantly, the tragic impasse of the
Victorian age.

In the final stanzas, the Tyrian Trader flees from the Greeks as the
scholar gipsy flees before European culture. He flees from the bearers
of 'culture' who will find no place for him in the world they are so light-
heartedly inaugurating.

When Tennyson's head had assimilated honest doubts to the edge of
scepticism, his 'heart stood up and answered "I have felt" '. When
Strauss had undermined the historicity of the Bible, he tried to reinstate
it as a myth. Matthew Arnold, also, tried to find an emotional cure for
the loss of faith, In his case, it took the form of an attempt to substitute
culture and poetry for religion, and to find a few axioms that could be
made real on the moral pulses. But when it came to the trial, his head
gained the day, honesty won the victory over expediency. 'The Scholar-
Gipsy' is a poem of unbelief. Arnold did not discover anything adequate
to replace the hopes of the earlier world.

Mr Wilson Knight himself believes (I take it) in what the scholar gipsy
symbolizes, and believes that that is a wisdom both complementary and
superior to the 'knowledge' of Oxford. That is, naturally, a possible
viewpoint to hold, but I believe that Arnold himself held an opposite
one, and that the organization of his poem is essentially part of the
Arnold world.

From 'The Last Enchantments', *Review of English Studies*, N.S.,
Vol. 8, 1957, pp. 257–65.

PAUL EDWARDS

# Hebraism, Hellenism, and
# *The Scholar-Gipsy*

. . . The fault with the Scholar-Gipsy is that he is a little too inactive to
give any impression of intellectual strength or to appeal as a human
figure (as distinct from the symbol which he becomes later on in the
poem) in his seventeenth-century setting. His most characteristic poses
are slack and lethargic:

> Trailing in the cool stream [his] fingers wet,
>     As the slow punt swings round:
> And leaning backwards in a pensive dream, . . .
>                     [1853 text throughout]

The threshers labour in the barn and, watching them, is the Scholar-
Gipsy 'hanging on a gate'. The children, even, are occupied collecting
cresses, and they

> Have known thee watching, all an April day,
>     The springing pastures and the feeding kine;
> And mark'd thee, when the stars come out and shine,
>     Through the long dewy grass move slow away.

He leaves the river bank when the reapers come to bathe there; he
dodges the smock-frocked boors at the ale house; and though he gives
flowers to the girls, he does not speak to them. His dress is 'outlandish',
his eyes are 'vague' as he stands 'Rapt, twirling in [his] hand a wither'd
spray', rather like an ineffectual magic wand, 'And waiting for the spark
from Heaven to fall'. The unworldliness is more than faintly irritating,
and one of the Scholar-Gipsy's most earnest defenders, Professor Wilson
Knight, admits himself unhappy about the word 'fall' here, with its
implication that there is no inner spark in the Scholar-Gipsy himself.[1]
'To be awakened' would, he suggests, have been better. But the word
suits the context. Like the withered spray, it suggests a certain hollowness in the Scholar-Gipsy's way of life, an aimlessness reinforced by the
use of 'waiting' and 'twirling' here. The contrast between energy and
lethargy is perhaps brought out most strongly in the stanza which
describes the reapers:

[1] 'The Scholar-Gipsy: An Interpretation', *Review of English Studies*, N.S.
Vol. 6, 1955, pp. 53–62.

And, above Godstow Bridge, when hay-time's here
 In June, and many a scythe in sunshine flames,
    Men, who through those wide fields of breezy grass
 Where black-wing'd swallows haunt the glittering Thames,
    To bathe in the abandoned lasher pass,
       Have often pass'd thee near
 Sitting upon the river bank o'ergrown:
    Mark'd thy outlandish garb, thy figure spare,
    Thy dark vague eyes, and soft abstracted air;
       But, when they came from bathing, thou wert gone.

The immediacy of 'hay-time's here', the scythes flaming in the sun, the swallows darting over 'the glittering Thames', the reapers and 'those wide fields of breezy grass' which they are cutting present a picture of vitality and charm, in which men are seen as having mastered nature without spoiling it. If the Scholar-Gipsy's contemplation could be seen to have a place in this picture, all might be well, yet he is shown to be isolated from it. In contrast to the reaped fields is 'the river bank o'ergrown', its atmosphere that of the older Gothic or graveyard school of poetry, where the hero sits shunning the company of men. Yet only in the second half of the poem does the Scholar-Gipsy's isolation have much point, as a symbol for the Victorian reader who has something much more distinct and quite different to escape from.

It appears that there are two very different kinds of escape involved here, and that one of the weaknesses of the poem is its failure to offer a satisfactory motive for the actual escape of the Scholar-Gipsy from his own age, as distinct from his symbolic escape from the Victorian age. That Arnold was himself dissatisfied with the poem is shown by the well-known letter to Clough:

> I am glad you like the 'Gipsy-Scholar'—but what does it *do* for you? Homer *animates*—Shakespeare *animates*—in its own poor way I think 'Sohrab and Rustum' *animates*—the Gipsy-scholar at best awakens a pleasing melancholy. But this is not what we want.
>
> > The complaining millions of men
> > Darken in labour and pain—
>
> what they want is something to *animate* and *ennoble* them—not merely to add zest to their melancholy or grace to their dreams.[2]

This seems to argue in favour of what we have already noticed, a curiously enervating condition in the Scholar-Gipsy's life. The business of knowing is made to seem too negative, too inert, too much a matter of 'waiting for the spark'. What Arnold needed for his time was a symbol of intellectual vigour, as the reader of *Culture and Anarchy* will recognize, but what the Scholar-Gipsy turns out to be is a symbol

---

[2] *Letters of M. Arnold to A. H. Clough*, ed. H. F. Lowry, 1932, p. 146 (30 November 1853).

of physical lethargy and intellectual passiveness, probably under the influence of Arnold's enthusiasm for the *Bhagavad Gita*. Had any irony been traceable in the poem, it might have appeared that Arnold had become dissatisfied with his hero as a symbolic figure, actually in the process of composition, and that this had led him to substitute in the final stanzas the Tyrian Trader, who, though an analogy is drawn between him and the Scholar-Gipsy in the poem, is in fact a quite different sort of figure. But the irony is not apparent, which suggests that the conflict was taking place below the surface of Arnold's consciousness, a conflict, which is later to be the subject of *Culture and Anarchy* and a constantly recurring theme of Arnold's letters, between Hellenism or knowing and Hebraism or doing.

That this conflict could still lead to incoherence many years after the composition of 'The Scholar-Gipsy' is apparent in the early pages of *Culture and Anarchy*.[3] Within two pages, Arnold makes two seemingly contradictory observations:

> Religion says: *The Kingdom of God is within you;* and culture, in like manner, places human perfection in an *internal* condition. (p. 47) Perfection, as culture conceives it, is not possible while the individual remains isolated. The individual is required, under pain of being stunted and enfeebled in his own development if he disobeys, to carry others along with him in his march towards perfection, to be continually doing all he can to enlarge and increase the volume of the human stream sweeping thitherwards. (p. 49).

The first quotation describes the state of the Scholar-Gipsy, but the second, even allowing for his unconvincing claim that his gipsy wisdom 'when fully learned [he] will to the world impart', is quite unlike his deliberate seeking of isolation from other men. This quotation suggests, in fact, that it is not possible to dissociate contemplation wholly from action, as the Scholar-Gipsy tries to do. Essentially, the Scholar-Gipsy has the Hellenist qualities:

> Hellenism, and human life in the hands of Hellenism, is invested with a kind of aërial ease, clearness and radiancy, they are kept full of sweetness and light. Difficulties are kept out of view, and the beauty and rationalness of the ideal have all our thoughts. (p. 134)

But against this, Hellenism has its imperfections:

> The Renascence, that great re-awakening of Hellenism . . . had, like the anterior Hellenism of the pagan world, a side of moral weakness, and of relaxation or insensibility of the moral fibre. (p. 141).

And so, as a result of these weaknesses:

> As we said of the former defeat of Hellenism, if Hellenism was defeated, this shows that Hellenism was imperfect, and that its ascen-

[3] *Culture and Anarchy*, ed. J. Dover Wilson, Cambridge, 1931.

dency at that moment would not have been for the world's good.
(pp. 142–3).

Arnold ends by coming out strongly in favour of an infusion of Hellenism
into his own over-Hebraistic age, arguing that just as Hellenism was in
the past 'not for the world's good', so it is with Hebraism in the present.
Hebraism in itself is not condemned by Arnold, except when it is un-
tempered by the 'sweetness and light' of Hellenism. At its best, Arnold
tells us, it has qualities which Hellenism lacks. 'Hebraism', he writes,
'—and here is the source of its wonderful strength—has always been
severely preoccupied with the impossibility of being at ease in Zion'
(p. 135). So Arnold's conclusion is that Hebraism and Hellenism, doing
and knowing, must in the end be reconciled, 'and thus man's two great
natural forces . . . will no longer be dissociate and rival, but will be a
joint force of right thinking and strong doing to carry him on to perfection' (p. 207).

Arnold's correspondence reveals the same strong impulse on occasions
towards Hebraistic 'activity'. In 1852, the year before the publication
of the poem, he writes that 'the world might do worse than dismiss too
high pretentions, and settle down on what it can see and handle and
appreciate'. Though, despite our struggles, the world deteriorates, he
adds, 'still, nothing can absolve us from the duty of doing all we can to
keep alive our courage and activity'.[4] This word 'activity' occurs often
in the letters in a favourable sense. Later in the letter to Clough quoted
above which asks of 'The Scholar-Gipsy' 'what does it *do* for you?',
Arnold tells his friend, 'you certainly do not seem to me sufficiently to
desire and earnestly strive towards—assured knowledge—activity—
happiness. You are too content to fluctuate—to be for ever learning,
never coming to the knowledge of the truth. That is why, with you, I
feel it necessary to stiffen myself and hold fast my rudder'. There are
several things here which recall 'The Scholar-Gipsy', and the word
'activity' and the phrase 'to stiffen myself and hold fast my rudder'
suggest those qualities which we found lacking in the Scholar-Gipsy,
yet which appear in the Tyrian Trader, that man of action who
'snatched his rudder and shook out more sail, And day and night held
on indignantly . . .', a surprising substitute, even in an epic simile, for
the gentle Scholar-Gipsy. In another letter, written in 1854, only a year
after the poem was published, Arnold comments on the Oxford
countryside:

> I got up alone into one of those little coombs that papa was so fond
> of and which I had in my mind in the 'Gipsy-Scholar', and felt the
> peculiar *sentiment* of this country and neighbourhood as deeply as
> ever. But I am much struck with the apathy and *poorness* of the people
> here as they now strike me, and their petty, pottering habits compared
> with the students of Paris, of Germany, or even of London. Anima-
> tion and interest and the power of work seems so sadly wanting in

[4] *Letters of Arnold to Clough*, pp. 122–3 (7 June 1852).

them . . . However, we must hope that the coming changes and the infusion of Dissenters' sons of that muscular, hardworking unblasé middle class—for it is that in spite of its abominable disagreeableness —may brace the flaccid sinews of Oxford a little.[5]

About ten years later, a year or two before the publication of *Culture and Anarchy*, he is writing of the Italians:

> The Piedmontese is the only virile element—he is like a country Frenchman—but he is small leaven to leaven the whole lump. And the whole lump want backbone, serious energy and the power of honest work to a degree that makes one impatient . . . the Italians are no more civilised by virtue of their refinement alone than we are civilised by virtue of our energy alone.[6]

This last sentence, I think, sums up what many readers feel to be wrong with 'The Scholar-Gipsy' and its hero, and what Arnold appears to have felt himself when he asked 'what does it *do* for you?', this lack of what he calls variously 'backbone', 'activity', 'serious energy', 'power of honest work' and so on, which, for all Arnold's feeling for the *Bhagavad Gita* and its quietism, makes the answer of 'The Scholar-Gipsy' to the problems of the modern world an imperfect one. Mr V. S. Seturaman[7] points out that we cannot ignore the influence of Hindu literature and thought upon Arnold, and argues that 'The Scholar-Gipsy' proposes the supreme step of the *Bhagavad Gita*, the rejection of action and all its fruits. He sees 'The Scholar-Gipsy' as essentially Oriental, in reaction against the West. He quotes from a letter written by Arnold in 1848, to Clough to whom he had lent a copy of the *Bhagavad Gita*:

> I am disappointed the Oriental wisdom, God grant it were mine, pleased you not. To the Greeks, foolishness.[8]

But I think no reader of *Culture and Anarchy* could see in this early iso-lated quotation a rejection of Hellenism—it is, more likely, a glancing aside, away from the great Hellenist tradition, to 'the side of moral weakness' of 'that anterior Hellenism of the pagan world'. The Hellenism of Arnold is in fact close to the doctrine of the *Bhagavad Gita* in setting knowing above doing, and this aspect of both Hellenism and 'the Oriental wisdom' can be recognized in the Scholar-Gipsy. But Hebraism is always pressing its attentions on Arnold, so that the 'grave' Tyrian Trader's rejection of the 'lighthearted' Greeks is perhaps not the Orien-tal wisdom of the *Bhagavad Gita* so much as the Hebraic 'seriousness', allied in this case to images of the equally Hebraic 'activity'. Arnold

---

[5] *Letters of Matthew Arnold 1848–1888*, ed. G. W. E. Russell, 1901, Vol. I, pp. 44–5 (October 1854).

[6] *Ibid.*, Vol. I, pp. 325–6 (21 June 1865).

[7] 'The Scholar-Gipsy and Oriental Wisdom' (*R.E.S.*, N.S. Vol. 9, 1958, pp. 411–13).

[8] *Letters of Arnold to Clough*, p. 69 (1 March 1848).

could not, in the end, approve of the total rejection of action and its fruits, any more than he could rest content with a figure expressive of such an attitude. He was too much of a Hebraist at heart for that, and for him, as we have seen, the supreme step was 'a joint force of right thinking and strong doing'. For this reason I believe that the effect of the *Bhagavad Gita* on 'The Scholar-Gipsy' is to confuse the central issue between Hebraism and Hellenism and with this, the purpose of the poem, which appears to me to be their reconciliation. One cannot ignore this Hebraist side to Arnold's personality—one might call it his Inspector-of-Schools side—and I could multiply examples of it from his letters. For example there are his comments on Count Larisch, the Austrian Finance Minister—'an English gentleman of the best type in simplicity and honourableness, with more suavity, but without the backbone to save the Austrian finances; and he and all his class alarmingly without the *seriousness* which is so English, the faculty to appreciate thoroughly the gravity of a situation, to be thoroughly stirred by it, and to put their shoulders earnestly to the wheel in consequence'.[9] And as a final example, only six months after writing the letter to Clough about the Oriental wisdom Arnold tells him 'I desire you should have some occupation—I think it desirable for everyone', adding that 'since the Baconian era wisdom is not to be found in deserts'.[10]

There are, then, two Arnolds to consider: there is the enthusiast for the best of Hellenism and the lover of Hindu literature and religion, the Arnold who was drawn to the figure of the Scholar-Gipsy; and there is the Arnold who recognized the strength of Hebraism in British life as well as its limitations, who realized that an overdose of Hellenism and the *Bhagavad Gita* could be as dangerous to British society as the overdose of Hebraism from which he saw it as currently suffering. His attitude to the Scholar-Gipsy at the time of the poem's composition has been hinted at in the letter in which Arnold describes the Oxfordshire countryside and says that he 'felt the peculiar *sentiment* of this country and neighbourhood as deeply as ever', but goes on to complain about the 'petty, pottering habits' of the students there, and of the need for 'animation and interest and the power of work'. The two Arnolds are there, as they are in his description of his feeling for the Middle Ages:

> I have a strong sense of the irrationality of that period, and of the utter folly of those who take it seriously and play at restoring it, still, it has poetically the greatest charm and refreshment for me.[11]

These words might almost have been written of the world of the Scholar-Gipsy.

But now to return to the poem—up to line 120 the Scholar-Gipsy has been seen, not by Arnold himself, but according to report, enjoying the

---

[9] *Letters of Matthew Arnold*, Vol. I, pp. 353–4 (30 September 1865).
[10] *Letters of Arnold to Clough*, p. 88 (12 August 1848).
[11] *Letters of Matthew Arnold*, Vol. I, p. 147 (17 December 1860).

kind of eternal week-end which put Leavis off the poem.[12] But in the next stanza, Arnold questions whether he has not in fact seen the Scholar-Gipsy himself 'in winter, on the causeway chill . . . battling with the snow' and struggling 'towards Hinksey and its wintry ridge'. The description of the Scholar-Gipsy's life has moved through spring (l. 57), summer (l. 88) and autumn (l. 111) when suddenly the 'week-end' is over, and Arnold sees the Scholar-Gipsy in the world of reality where life and nature compel him to battle with the storm. This new vision of the Scholar-Gipsy prefigures that of the other battler, the Tyrian Trader. We are led from this point to the Scholar-Gipsy's death, and his rebirth as a symbol for the Victorian age, yet he fails to serve satisfactorily as this chiefly because he has been so strongly established in the early part of the poem as a contemplative. Quotation from *Culture and Anarchy* and the letters has shown that, for Arnold, contemplation without action is not enough. As a result, Arnold allows the Scholar-Gipsy to run for cover—

> Fly hence, our contact fear!
> Still fly, plunge deeper in the bowering wood!

—allows him to 'emerge' into his former paradise, still 'hanging on a gate'—

> . . . and resting on the moonlit pales,
> Freshen thy flowers, as in former years,

and at once proceeds to the epic simile which introduces the new hero, the Tyrian Trader, whose resemblance to the Scholar-Gipsy is quite superficial. The Scholar-Gipsy, prone in his punt, 'trailing in the cool stream [his] fingers wet' is only very loosely analogous to the Tyrian Trader who

> . . . snatch'd his rudder, and shook out more sail,
>   And day and night held on indignantly
> O'er the blue Midland waters with the gale,
>   Betwixt the Syrtes and soft Sicily,
>     To where the Atlantic raves
> Outside the Western Straits, and unbent sails
>   There, where down cloudy cliffs, through sheets of foam,
>   Shy traffickers, the dark Iberians come;
>     And on the beach undid his corded bales.

The images here are of vigorous, even violent action, of struggle and anger, and they contrast with the actions of the Scholar-Gipsy—except in Arnold's vision of him climbing towards Hinksey—by implying an involvement in, not a withdrawal from, the problems of the time in the very process of escaping from the problems. The 'merry' and 'light-hearted' Greeks from whom the Tyrian Trader turns might cause some trouble to those who find them unsatisfactory equivalents to the 'sick

[12] F. R. Leavis, *Revaluation*, 1936, pp. 186–91.

fatigue' of the Victorian world which they are supposed to parallel. But admitting the looseness of the equation here—this is, after all, an epic simile—I doubt if Arnold looked upon these Greeks with complete approval. They may remind us of that 'anterior Hellenism of the pagan world' with its 'side of moral weakness', and though they have their attractions, their 'amber grapes and Chian wine, Green bursting figs and tunnies steeped in brine' could represent an over-indulgence in the senses that is, in a way, the weakness of the Scholar-Gipsy too. Certainly they are 'lighthearted', but this was not a quality that met with Arnold's unqualified approval. We have recognised the stress which he places on the need for 'seriousness' to be joined with the 'sweetness and light' of Hellenism. This seriousness is not the same thing as 'melancholy', the 'pleasing melancholy' of the Scholar-Gipsy which he said was 'not enough' for this too has its side of indulgence and moral weakness, but rather the 'serious energy' lacked by the Italians, the 'seriousness which is so English' lacked by Count Larisch, the 'serious conception of righteousness' lacked according to a letter written in 1871 by Greece, Rome, fifteenth-century Italy and nineteenth-century France.[13] So, in the second part of the poem, we are shown first an idealized Hindu-Hellene fleeing from Victorian Hebraism, and then an idealized Hebraist fleeing from 'the anterior Hellenism of the pagan world'. The best of both worlds is shown in flight from the worst, and I think we might conclude as Professor Wilson Knight does that Arnold is 'striving towards a fusion of two traditions, Western and Eastern', though the poem does not appear to effect this fusion successfully, probably because, as I have suggested before, much of the conflict is taking place below a conscious level. The poem might have been better had it moved more surely from the qualities and defects of these traditions towards the point of fusion in the figure of the Tyrian Trader; as it is, it gropes uncertainly, presenting ironical possibilities without the irony. But the conflict of the poem is an old one in the romantic tradition and F. W. Bateson has observed it in the work of earlier nineteenth-century poets:

> It is essentially this conflict, between the personality integrated into a social environment and the anti-social split man . . . that is mirrored in Romantic poetry. In so far as the poetry was in the central tradition of Romanticism, the split-man was its hero and society was its villain. But in so far as the poetry was *poetry* . . . the issue had to appear to hang in the balance. The hero (the ideal) must not win too easily; the villain (social reality) must be given a chance. And so, by curious paradox, to be a good romantic poet you had to know the case against Romanticism. You had to be a rationalist as well as an irrationalist, a functioning member of society as well as a social revolutionary or a social escapist.[14]

---

[13] *Letters of Matthew Arnold*, Vol. 2, pp. 55–6 (31 January 1871).
[14] F. W. Bateson, *English Poetry: A Critical Introduction*, 1950, pp. 195–6.

The final impression of the poem, it appears to me, is of 'confused alarms of struggle and flight', for Arnold still has not resolved truly whether the good man must do battle with his age and risk contagion, or flee from it and risk being 'stunted and enfeebled'. Too much stress is laid in the early part on the Scholar-Gipsy himself, a figure which appeals so strongly to one side of Arnold's nature that it becomes disproportionately significant. As a result, this stress on the Scholar-Gipsy becomes a sort of indulgence on Arnold's part in 'pleasing melancholy', which he found himself to be a serious wea! ness in the poem. The structure and argument of the poem, which should be working towards the kind of fusion described above, is slackened and its purpose obscured by Arnold's excursion into a field of personal sentiment which, to a certain degree, is at odds with his intellectual conviction. The poem gropes towards its resolution, yet with the introduction of the Tyrian Trader, confidence seems to come, and it is not surprising that so many readers find the last two stanzas the most satisfying and effective in the poem. But the resolution is still not wholly satisfying because, like a mother with two screaming children, Arnold seems to be saying 'All right, you can *both* win'.

From 'Hebraism, Hellenism, and "The Scholar-Gipsy" ', *Durham University Journal*, Vol. 54, N.S. Vol. 23, 1962, pp. 121–7, (122–7).

# *Thyrsis*

. . . 'The Scholar-Gipsy' involves a dream of being from the world of becoming and leaves undetermined whether the dream was a delusion. 'Thyrsis' devotes itself to recovering a vision of being from the world of becoming and insists that it is true. Both dream and vision derive from a response to the features of the landscape.

The Cumnor poems exemplify the frequently discussed move in Arnold from what may be called uncertainty whether his dreams pass through the gate of horn or of ivory to a conviction that his dreams are all of horn. Severely qualified though it was, the greater optimism of Arnold's later work is unquestionable: the two Obermann poems provide another clear example. The twentieth century has found, with Tennysonian authority, the expression of doubt more satisfyingly honest than the expression of assurance, however tentatively it may be offered. In itself this is a quite invalid criterion. We must allow a poet his faith or his doubt, and ask only that it be properly realized in his poem. Proper realization means in this context the due rendering of the Cumnor countryside so that it really seems, at least for the duration of the poem, to contain the truths it is said to contain.

The problem is the signal tree, not, certainly, whether it was oak or elm, truly solitary or near a clump of pines, on Cumnor Hurst or just above Chilswell Farm, visible or not visible on the path from South or North Hinksey.[1] The problem is whether the tree can do the work the poem asks it to do. It is important to pay careful attention to what is first said of the tree, for on that saying the poem will depend. The main details are given in the third stanza after a brief mention of the tree in the second:

> That single elm-tree bright
> Against the west—I miss it! is it gone?
> We prized it dearly; while it stood, we said,
> Our friend, the Gipsy-Scholar, was not dead;
> While the tree lived, he in these fields lived on. (ll. 26–30)

What, it is pertinent to ask, was their authority for this assurance? More accurately, it is impertinent to ask the question at this point; it only becomes pertinent in the subsequent development of the poem.

---

[1] The various candidates are reviewed by Sir Francis Wylie in an essay on 'The Scholar-Gipsy Country' contributed to *Commentary*, pp. 351–73, esp. pp. 356–60.

Thus early, the assurance emerges as a youthful fancy, slightly whimsical perhaps, and therefore all the more amenable to that easy nostalgia for happiness past which the poem so largely exploits. If the poem proceeded merely to exploit that nostalgia, it would not matter that no authority is given for the assurance; it would, indeed, be quite proper. Quite proper, that is, if the eventual sight of the tree signalled only the memorial recovery in the evening of life of the joyous hopes of the morning.[2] Such a poem would have no doubt been as charming as the poem Arnold actually wrote; it would have hung together rather better, and have been quite commonplace. But that is not the poem which Arnold wrote.

The lines of what Arnold is about are clear enough, even if there are more of them than there are in 'The Scholar-Gipsy'. 'Thyrsis' extends the earlier poem's concern with the possibility of belief in unbelieving times into a search for confirmation that the possibility is well founded, for confirmation that the hopes and creative ability of youth are recoverable in age. The search is rendered in terms of literal passage through a landscape which shows almost everywhere the evidence of change, the cycle of becoming, and the evocation by way of pastoral convention of a changelessly immortal landscape. The search is for evidence in the landscape of becoming that it is a copy, however imperfect, of the landscape of being. If the search is successful it will confirm the existence of what Arnold a few years later was to call the eternal not ourselves which makes for righteousness, something identifiably outside the cycle of mortality which makes it both bearable and meaningful.[3]

In the youth of man and nature the pastoral mode embodied an effortlessly meaningful communication between this world and another. The continuity between becoming and being was assured by the beneficent rule of Proserpine, queen of the dead, who 'herself had trod Sicilian fields' (l. 93). Her head was crowned in the underworld with flowers which 'first open'd on Sicilian air' (l. 89), and this persistence of the emblems of life into the time of death confirmed that Orpheus could indeed have brought back Eurydice and that 'Moschus' was right to think he could emulate him on behalf of Bion (ll. 84–90). To this 'boon southern country' Thyrsis has gone in death to hear Daphnis sing the perils of life and the consolations of heaven: 'all the marvel of the golden skies' (ll. 175–90). As in the youth of man, so in the youth of Thyrsis and Corydon, rowing their skiff along 'the shy Thames shore', where the mowers 'stood with suspended scythe to see us pass', the emblems of arrested time in a world of time (ll. 126–29). But the

---

[2] See J. P. Curgenven, ' "Thyrsis" V: Art and Signification', *Litera*, Vol. 6, 1959; 'the quest in the poem is "less a *recherche du temps perdus* than a *recherche de l'absolu*".'

[3] The distinction between the immortal world of pastoral and the mortal world of Cumnor is recognized by Richard Giannone, 'The Quest Motif in "Thyrsis" ', *Victorian Poetry*, Vol. 3, 1965, pp. 71–80, who sees its importance in different terms from mine.

Cumnor hills are not Sicilian fields; Proserpine does not know them, and instead of her crown of living flowers there are only 'the coronals of that forgotten time', the long-gone flowers of 'the loved hill-side' (ll. 112–17). The passage of the seasons marks itself as surely on the landscape as the passage of the years on Corydon. In the 'winter-eve' of the poem's now (l. 16) only the primroses are left as 'orphans of the flowery prime' (l. 120). The dying of the year and the day, the death of Thyrsis, the ageing of Corydon, the passing of 'Sibylla' (l. 4), and even of those mowers who once held still their scythes lead inevitably to the quiet despair of *ubi sunt*? (ll. 121–30). The haunts which once mediated between mortality and immortality, which once permitted a dream of 'glad perennial youth,' can no longer work their magic. Corydon picks his way cautiously through the landscape—'runs it not here, the track by Childsworth Farm?' (l. 11)—seeking the missing tree. If that too is gone, then Corydon's youth with Thyrsis and all its hopes are as irretrievably past as Proserpine in Sicilian fields and Daphnis singing the Lityerses song. The vision of being is irrecoverable, and if so, even the loved hillside confirms the sad experience of growing older in the world away from Cumnor. The 'unbreachable' if 'long-batter'd' fortress of the world interposes its wall between Corydon and his youthful vision of the mountain-top throne of truth, bright and bare in his morning's sun (ll. 141–50), the very 'marvel of the golden skies' of which Daphnis now sings to Thyrsis in the 'boon southern country'. Of old there was 'easy access' to the grace of Proserpine (l. 91), but now 'long the way appears' to the airy throne of truth. The morning is long gone, and the night offers only repose, a cessation from earthly turmoil. From becoming to being involves passage across an 'unpermitted ferry's flow' (l. 85), absolute discontinuity with no mediator between.

'Alack, for Corydon,' indeed. But, in striving to emulate 'Sicilian shepherds' by 'piping a ditty sad' for a lost mate (ll. 81–84), he not only gives his 'grief its hour' (l. 102), he also renders clearly the difference between becoming and being, their erstwhile continuity and present separateness. We are theologically prepared to appreciate epiphany. It comes when, after painful and unsuccessful striving to recover the past, he is suddenly startled by an unexpected repetition of the past into the instinctive move which renews it. 'A troop of Oxford hunters going home, / As in old days' drives him to flight (ll. 153–54), just as, in those 'old days', they had driven the Scholar Gipsy. And so the tree. It stands there in the world of becoming, 'bare on its lonely ridge' (l. 160), backed by the sun which in 'life's morning' had shone so brightly on the bare mountain top of truth. It is now an evening sun and night will soon follow, but between Corydon and the immortality after death, between becoming and being, there is the tree signalling that not all things change, that some things abide to body forth to the world of becoming the permanence of being. Such embodiment is no longer the bright, bare summit which presented itself to 'the less practised eye of sanguine youth' (l. 142), but a tree backed by a sky which is 'orange and pale violet' (l. 159), orange to remind of the bright sun of morning youth, and pale violet to foreshadow night and death. And then the vision is gone, a 'fugitive and gracious light' indeed, which we are soon told the Scholar Gipsy also seeks in these hills, and so does Corydon, and so did Thyrsis (ll. 201–11). Their youthful poetry was right, after all; the 'rustic flute' piped of permanent truths in a world of cross doubts and shifting cares. The 'haunt beloved' which seemed so changed at first is now shown to yield a virtue still (l. 220), and the poem can end with a whispered assurance from Thyrsis to Corydon, the full establishment of communication between immortality and mortality, being and becoming, validated by the persistence of the tree and the Scholar, those mediators between the two realms.

But an elm is a tree, a vegetable, and no more than an oak or sequoia is it evidence of permanence. Longevity, it must be said, is not the same as immortality: it is not even a mortal approximation of immortality. We are insistently reminded of the discrepancy, if we are at all awake, by the poem's very emphasis upon the vegetable indices of impermanence. The poem buckles beneath the weight of its own philosophic pretensions. To hold together it must find something, preferably in the landscape, to mediate between the literal world of the Cumnor hills with all its emotional associations and the idyllically unchanging world of the antique pastoral. So a tree which begins as the unexplained fancy of youth ends as arbitrary sign, an allegorical object in a literal landscape,[4] but the 'justification' for the sign remains the unexplained fancy. Arnold, it seems, had long forgotten the shite's oracle on the unpoetical attributes of the allegorical. If he had recalled it, he might have paused before exclaiming 'I cannot reach the signal-tree to-night' (l. 165). We see what he means, of course. He has been afforded the maximum vision that mortal can look for in these bad times, and he rests content, for Arnold was never extravagant in his optimism. He has just devoted three stanzas to a careful reminder that morning is youth, evening is age, and night is death; indeed such an identification of the diurnal with the human cycle is central to the poem, and perhaps explains why, in contrast with 'The Scholar-Gipsy', there are no night pieces among the remembered scenes of youth. So the fact that he cannot reach the tree to-night 'means' that he cannot reach it in this life: mediators between being and becoming can in their very nature only be glimpsed at moments and from a distance. But the exclamation also irresistibly reminds us that all this is a nostalgic outing commenced a little too late in the day. If the tree still stands, it can be inspected the next morning or some other

[4] Wylie's own conviction, *Commentary*, pp. 356–57, endorsing the view of 'generations of Oxford men', that the signal-elm was really an oak, which could not have looked 'on Ilsley Downs', as Corydon thought, because Boars Hill would be in the way, is an ironic comment upon the obstacles created for topographical source-hunting by placing a symbolic object in a literal landscape. The probability that the signal-tree never existed in its Arnoldian guise and place makes it, as mediator between becoming and being, even more fanciful than the poem itself indicates.

F

morning. But of course that would never do: the whole thrust of the poem makes the tree a symbol which is only complete when glimpsed against an 'orange and pale violet evening-sky'. The literal landscape very properly rebels against the symbolic burden it is forced to carry.

The poem's process is a familiar one in Arnold. The emotions associated with landscape seem satisfyingly resolved; the epicedium effects its due modulation from despair to consolatory hope. But the resolution depends upon a highly questionable metaphysics involving a fanciful association more expressive of feeling than thought and the arbitrary selection of one object from a literally rendered landscape as a symbolic sign. The poem's heart is stronger than its head. 'Thyrsis' is a less successful poem than 'The Scholar-Gipsy' because, while the earlier poem uses landscape in ways which accord with the poet's strength to render the emotional quality of generally presented kinds of life, the later poem does that and tries to do more, tries to use landscape to make precise distinctions between this world and another. 'Thyrsis' is less successful because it fails to realize its greater philosophic ambitions.

A case might perhaps be made for preferring 'Thyrsis' just because it does try to be 'more important' than 'The Scholar-Gipsy'. But usually, one suspects, a preference for 'Thyrsis' signals a response to the strong heart it brings to the English countryside. The most strongly emotional portion of 'The Scholar-Gipsy' is the five stanzas of dismissal with which it ends, only one of which evokes the Cumnor hills and that in general terms. In the earlier description of the Scholar's haunts the speaker's—Arnold's—undoubted rural nostalgia rarely becomes overt, because it is passed through the dream concentration upon a gradually created figure. But in 'Thyrsis' the poet's nostalgia is overt and weighty, phrasing felicitously an experience which most have known, something charmingly commonplace. It tempts to hikes about 'the Scholar-Gipsy country', more accurately named 'the "Thyrsis" country', whose pleasures are to be set beside the search for Pickwickian inns or Wordsworth's tracks in the Lake District. The poem certainly asks more of us, is far from content merely to render the charmingly commonplace, but it is perhaps because it fails to be convincing in these endeavours that the track seems to run so clear from the Cumnor hills to the old vicarage at Grantchester. . . .

From *Arnold's Poetic Landscapes*, Johns Hopkins Press, Baltimore, 1969, pp. 224–9.

P. F. BAUM

# Stanza Form in *The Scholar-Gipsy* and *Thyrsis*

That 'The Scholar-Gipsy' and 'Thyrsis' are meant to be recognized as companion pieces and that Arnold hoped in 'Thyrsis' to repeat the success of the 'The Scholar-Gipsy' are obvious enough; but there are a few similarities between them which are not altogether obvious.

The stanza seems to have been original with Arnold. It has some likeness with that of Keats's 'To a Nightingale,' which goes $ababcde^5c^3$ $de^5$, and is a kind of truncated sonnet with the eight line shortened. Arnold's form is more subtle, for it has two different quatrains (*bcbc* and *deed*) and the shortened line is nearer the middle to give a neater balance. Further, the sixth or shortened line riming with the first ($abcbc^5a^3$) seems to make the first six lines a finished unit and to divide the stanza into two separate parts, yet does not, and thus the ear is pleasingly deceived. For only in three stanzas of the twenty-five of 'The Scholar-Gipsy' and in five of the twenty-four of 'Thyrsis' is there a full stop at the end of the sixth line, and in only seven more in the former poem and four more in the latter is there a strong pause there.

A very special device of Arnold's is the break at the end of the first line of the stanzas. In 'The Scholar-Gipsy' there is a strong pause at the end of the first line in six stanzas and a full stop in eight others. In 'Thyrsis' there is a strong pause in one stanza and a full stop in ten others.

A stylistic peculiarity of both poems (though Arnold is fond of it elsewhere) is the number of lines beginning with 'And'. 'The Scholar-Gipsy' has 54 such lines of the total 250. There are only two stanzas without them; three stanzas have five of them. The proportion is less in 'Thyrsis'; it has only 35 such lines out of the total 240 lines. So also for lines beginning with 'But'; 9 in the one and 7 in the other. (This is probably a quasi-Homeric trick, strongly favoured in 'Sohrab', with an increased frequency of 'But' in 'Balder Dead'.) 'Thyrsis,' however, compensates by the number of exclamation points. There are only four of its twenty-four stanzas without one (in the final printing) and one stanza (16) has seven of them! But in 'Thyrsis' Arnold was deliberately forcing the note. . . .

From Chapter 8 of *Ten Studies in the Poetry of Matthew Arnold*, Duke University Press, Durham N.C., 1958, pp. 107–8.

HARVEY KERPNECK

# *Rugby Chapel*

. . . The poem is almost a synopsis of Arnold's favourite imagery. The
imagery of light and darkness is one unifying device Arnold exploits
unmercifully, in fact. From the opening picture of the sombre chapel at
sunset 'solemn, unlighted, austere,' with its apparent affiliation with the
picture the bemused world possesses of the zealot, Thomas Arnold,
we are in a twilight world wherein distinctions between light and darkness are conventionally difficult to make, and Arnold soon implies,
conventionally erroneously made. The light and darkness of the poem
correspond, in other words, to the spiritual light and dark of men's
minds in England of this time, to the state of intellectual lethargy and
palsied faiths which Arnold summarizes brilliantly in referring to

> Those who with half-open eyes,
> Tread the border-land dim
> 'Twixt vice and virtue. . . .

As the poem continues, however, the imagery sweeps outward in ever
broader arcs, and it soon encompasses the weary traveller who is revealed by the lantern of the 'gaunt and taciturn host' of the inn at the
end of the journey. The traveller, Matthew Arnold himself, of course,
is in darkness almost infernal, as he replies conciliatingly to the host's
query about his absent travelling companions, 'Hardly ourselves we
fought through'. Beginning, in other words, with the physical dark of
the chapel at twilight unrelieved to the physical eye by any gleam of
light, the imagery moves outward to generalize on the wayward condition of men, and then inward to specify ruthlessly the spiritual
condition of Arnold's own soul. As Arnold himself is involved in the
darkness and as his intellect shirks the task meet and proper for it, of
making necessary discriminations between 'vice and virtue', the poet
demonstrates to us that he can see himself as culpable as the worst, and
his pretensions being higher, as even darker of hue. The imagery of
light and dark is used, then, to establish the deceitfulness of common,
careless distinctions, even among aspiring spirits, and to establish
Arnold's contrition for his behaviour in the past, which seems to him
positively loathsome now. And, then recurring to the figure of his father
who lies buried in that sombre-seeming edifice, Arnold recognizes that
it is by contrast that his past has been ignoble, by contrast with the
selflessness of his father, a 'beacon of hope', that his perverse egoism,
the denial of his gift and his talent, seem so ludicrous. And the poem

concludes with the City of God shining luminously before the way-farers, thrusting on now under the aegis of such as Thomas Arnold, triumphant spirits now including Matthew Arnold, whose eyes have been completely opened, among them.

To say this thus summarily is, of course, to falsify to a degree, and to ignore a good deal of the light-dark imagery. But it does suggest to what use the imagery is put, and how Arnold uses it both to abase himself publicly and then to suggest the source of his renewal. To readers who remember 'Thyrsis' it has a further significance, as it suggests, in highly concentrated form, the use Arnold made of the 'light' sought by Thyrsis and Corydon and finally seen, in that poem. But, except that the use of this imagery here seems much less forced and both more all-pervading and more instrumental in carrying the theme, and a kind of perfection, of which its use in 'Thyrsis' is but a first draft, there might seem to be nothing gained in connecting the two poems by means of it. But of another of the principal images in 'Rugby Chapel' this cannot be said.

This is the image of the quest. Some considerable scholarship has been expended on examining Arnold's use of this image in various poems, of which a good example might be Dwight Culler's sensitive remarks in his valuable introduction to the Riverside selections. But no effort has been made to demonstrate how relentlessly Arnold exploited this image, in all its possible manifestations, how deliberately he worked over it in poem after poem, compelling it to bear a dozen different burdens, and finally distilling its essence into 'Rugby Chapel'. For the truth is, that a pattern in the use of this image can be discerned in the great spiritual poems, particularly in 'The Scholar-Gipsy', 'Stanzas from the Grande Chartreuse', and 'Thyrsis', a meaningful pattern which finds its logical fulfilment in 'Rugby Chapel'.

In 'The Scholar-Gipsy', Arnold forethoughtfully announces to his public his determination to make the image of the quest (which he names) a vehicle for his public exorcism of the demon of cynicism and unbelief which plagues him. He uses the image to convey to his readers a sense of the spiritual journey he has undertaken and a glimpse of the pass to which it has brought him—if I can continue this image, a narrow defile between towering doubts, doubts as to his own capacity for accomplishing anything permanent in the renovation of human nature or human society (see his insistence upon enrolling himself among the debilitated in spirit), doubts as to the efficacy of the present modes of resuscitating worn spirits, doubts as to the potential that still remains in what he sees as a decaying land. The quest which he undertakes, a veritable physical one through the lush Oxford countryside, brings him inexorably to the condition of England (Hades, conveyed in the Dido and Aeneas episode) and his own disconsolate state:

And then thy glad perennial youth would fade,
Fade and grow old at last, and die like ours.

And what has been actually the framework for the events in the poem, the ramble cross-country, has also been made the surrogate for Arnold's wrathful and uncomfortable enquiry into England's (and, consequently, his own) lack of grace.

In 'Stanzas from the Grande Chartreuse', there is a distinctly different use made of the image, which again, however, provides a backbone to the poem. The extracting of *exempla* from the manifestations of it is more blatant, the urgency with which it is made to suggest a spiritual condition more obvious. 'Stanzas' is *the* poem, if any poem can be singled out, in which Arnold faces his problem and demonstrates his unease at being unable to resolve it. The image, basically, provides the poem with that undertone of irony which makes it either suspicious or abhorrent to some scholars. Here the image is given the guise of a pilgrimage in which Arnold is the pilgrim journeying to the heights, in order, despite himself, to make contact with divinity, if only to find some vestige of it there and worship that. The result is neither elation nor deflation, but a realization that the journey is madness since the heights are an illusion. In other words, Arnold involves with the quest image his favourite theme of the discrepancy between the seeming and the real, and his counters, the Carthusian monks in their abode, Arnold himself, and the worldly without the gates, are enmeshed in a kind of multiple irony which casts a wide variety of illuminations on all their efforts and pretensions. The faith of the Carthusians is seen to be a dangerous anachronism (the illusion of the heights), Arnold's cynicism (his melancholy) and his half-hearted search for certitude are both derided, and the world, for its part, pictured as a lure, full of seeming pomp but largely inflated vanity and better eschewed. But, most significant of all, in the end this quest brings Arnold not, as in 'The Scholar-Gypsy' to hurling anathemas, but to the intuition that to dispel illusions may be gratifying, but hardly either nourishing or fructifying. In other words, pushing on, the quest deliberately begun in 'The Scholar-Gipsy' and which ended there with a glimpse of hell on earth, finds Arnold at the close of 'Stanzas' acknowledging what Faustus finally learnt, that 'where we are is hell', acknowledging, in other words, that it is an inward deprivation, and not an external condition, which has first to be remedied before 'all can be made new'.

The use of the quest image, then, takes on another, vastly more significant dimension, in 'Stanzas', when irony is super-added and the kind of egoism which is displayed in 'The Scholar-Gipsy', in which it is thought to be the world's corruption which abases the poet, becomes henceforth impossible. Arnold's opinion of the world alters very little, of course, but his sense of his own implication in its guilt is enormously reinforced. In 'Thyrsis', the quest image is again central, the poem is again structured along a journey (once again through the Oxford countryside—perhaps as a token of Arnold's feeling of returning to himself), and the journey is at once both inward and spiritual and palpable and physical. That there is another dimension here too is obvious, for it is a journey as well into consequences, if I might so put it, as the whole poem is an experiment in what ought to be an outworn mode, the pastoral. As the poem progresses, and Arnold traverses the Oxford hills seeking the signal-elm (the token to him and Clough of the reality of the vagrant vision of the Scholar-Gipsy), Arnold passes also through fluctuating moods of effort and deflation—suggested by the cutting in and out of the pastoral conventions. And when effort triumphs in the famous lines

> Well! wind-dispersed and vain the words will be,
>     Yet, Thyrsis, let me give my grief its hour
> In the old haunt, and find our tree-topp'd hill!
>     Who, if not I, for questing here hath power?

Arnold has forever crossed his Rubicon. For the first time, the quest is not only apparently successful, but actually so: Arnold acquiesces gratefully in the vision of the elm, and, although he 'cannot reach the signal-tree to-night,' he knows that what he seeks, and what he has so long sought, rather too often desultorily rather than fervently, is actually there. How he accomplishes this is simply by denying despair. By realizing at last fully the inevitable consequences of the kind of lethargy to which he has been subject, he has been released from its thrall. Once the inward vision had been attained, the chains that made his journey such a halting, frustrating, enervating one fell away.

In 'Thyrsis', then, for the first time the quest image is used to herald an affirmation, one might almost say an annunciation. That this affirmation was complete is evident in the way Arnold clothes his final statements in the poem's closing lines in pastoral array. What this signifies can be seen by comparing this ending with that of 'Stanzas', where Arnold embraces an abhorred relic of the past with distaste, convinced only that it is easier and no less reprehensible to do this than to succumb to the clamouring world. In 'Thyrsis', on the other hand, although the 'world's markets' are deplored no less (more defiantly, in fact), Arnold accepts and is illumined by a symbol of universal meaning, stretching back through pre-history to the shadow world of myth and forward to an illimitable future. There is no rejection of 'archaisms', but rather an insistent demonstration that he now realizes that such terms of scorn are futile and useless.

From the affirmation with which 'Thyrsis' concludes it is only a short step to 'Rugby Chapel', which is, I am suggesting, a retrospective account of another aspect of Arnold's liberation from scepticism and doubt. The imagery of the quest attains its final form in this poem. It is, as it was in 'Thyrsis', the vehicle not of a question but of its answer, not of uncertainty but of conviction. And what makes the climactic position of 'Rugby Chapel' in this series of great spiritual poems so obvious is, in fact, the way in which the image of the quest is used. In the first place, the quest is no longer solitary: although at one point in the poem, Arnold is shown on his journey alone, this picture is soon demonstrated

to belong to a past which has been destroyed, which has been shown up
for the delusion it was. And as the poem proceeds toward its victorious
close, the number of participants in the quest seems to increase, almost
visibly by individuals—because Arnold's concern is here almost for
the first time with the individual and not with the 'populace'—until
finally it is an army that moves across the burning sands of the world's
temptations toward the City of God. The difference between the use
of the image here and its use in previous poems, in at least this one
respect corresponds exactly to the nature of Arnold's achieved vision: it
is as a natural corollary of the vision of 'Thyrsis', which, in the form it
takes on here, is the fullest assimilation of his father's significance,
that the quest becomes a universal and not a lonely one. In the second
place, the quest is other-directed in still another way: Arnold's father's
devotion to his Christian function becomes the symbol of the quest for
an answer. Not Arnold's own jostling among doubts, but his father's
assured progress toward vindication, is made the equivalent of the quest
image, and, Arnold sees now it provides not only a fuller but a richer
equivalent. If man's life is a quest from birth, and if he, indeed, moves
inexorably from one mystery to another, how much more meaningful
the quest infused with that holy triad of faith, love, and hope than that
other filled with mistrust, dissatisfaction, and complacency which had
been Arnold's primary image! How much nobler an effigy of man's life
is the active, philanthropic Christian than the withdrawn, melancholy
one!

But it is not the differences alone in the use of the quest image here
which suggest how properly 'Rugby Chapel' belongs at this terminal
point on Arnold's spiritual journey; the similarities are significant, too.
In the first place, once again Arnold has involved the quest image with
the theme of illusion, the illusion . . . about Rugby Chapel and its
occupant, and, as we can now see, the illusion, secondly, about Arnold's
own career, which seems to him now to have been swathed in illusion.
In the second place, there are deliberate echoes of the landscapes, the
spiritual conditions they signified, from the earlier poems. In fact, most
of the poem and of the quest imagery in it, would seem to be a kind of
dramatization of that bleakly abstract description of faltering energies in
lines 141–151 of 'Thyrsis'. The description of the impregnable fastness
of Truth in those lines is caught up here and expanded into the three
linked pictures of the improper, the proper and the glorious future,
concerted approaches to that fastness. And, one part of the poem that
dealing, wholly in terms of the quest image (lines 72–123, the confrontation with St Peter), with Arnold's spiritual blindness in the past,
is an obvious parody of the passage from 'Thyrsis', which was an
apparently sober apologia for spiritual lassitude. From his new vantage-
point, Arnold is able to mock his vanity, almost with a masochistic
pleasure—like the flagellant's in his ecstasy. Another significant
'echo' of the use of the image in previous poems is heard in this same
passage. It is the repetition from 'Thyrsis' and 'Stanzas' of the picture of

the quest of man through upland rocks and bleak mountain wildernesses·
And again the imagery here seems to be a deliberate commentary upon
its appearances and meanings there. Whereas in 'Stanzas' the
mountains were aloof and forbidding, really the abode of death, and
the way through them led, not to assurances but to a bitter conundrum,
and whereas in 'Thyrsis', at first the mountains seem insuperable, and,
although later reduced to their proper dimensions, still at the end
confront the traveller with the prospect of treachery and perhaps
disappointment to come, here, in 'Rugby Chapel', they are the token
of an opportunity. Almost in the manner of Browning, Arnold demonstrates here a faith in the maxim that discouragement breeds faith and
hardihood. The 'rocks of the world' are seen to possess a function
ordained from on high, and the passage through them (in a line
deliberately reminiscent, perhaps, of one in 'Isolation') of the host, is
seen to be similarly ordained:

> —A God
> Marshall'd them, gave them their goal.

Of course, the echoes from the earlier poems, particularly the great
spiritual poems, are, in general, one of the clearest indications of the
terminal position of 'Rugby Chapel', and, if it were pertinent, I could
suggest how numerous they are. But one example, related to the use of
the image of the quest, will have to serve to demonstrate that this kind
of investigation could be extended to many other areas of the poem. I
have already quoted that disconcerting close to 'Stanzas from the Grande
Chartreuse', in which Arnold embraces the wasteland of a self-pitying
disillusionment, while, by implication, acknowledging how grudgingly
he does so, and that he realizes how little succour can be expected from
the desert sands. That conclusion, with its calculated insult to the old
faith, is a memorable one, and Arnold knew the impact with which it
would be felt by his readers, themselves at this time vitally concerned
with these same questions, and, with minor versions cf them, the
Manning fiasco, the Achilli trial, and so on, fresh in memory, even less
sympathetic than Arnold to what the Carthusians symbolized. Since
'Rugby Chapel' seems intended as an utter refutation of 'Stanzas', an
equally memorable and pithy close was necessary for it, preferably one
which formally annulled the thesis of 'Stanzas' as the whole poem did
*in extenso*. Arnold did, poetically, the wisest thing possible. Picking up
the very image with which 'Stanzas' concluded, he concluded this poem
with the army of mankind struggling, yearning towards its new
Jerusalem:

> On, to the *bounds* of the waste,
> On, to the City of God.

Although this 'waste' is not the desert of 'Stanzas'—for that was
Arnold's own dejection and this is the wasteland of fatigue, poverty and,
undoubtedly, the accumulated noxious orthodoxies of servile men—the

reminiscence of the previous usage would arise for the reader. The reader would take his sense of the meaning of the reminiscence from the different attitudes of the characters in the two pictures, in the earlier one supine in despair, in this newly risen physically and spiritually, grasping towards the high, white star of Truth.

But perhaps the clearest indication of 'Rugby Chapel's' place in this sequence of spiritual masterpieces is neither the changes rung on the quest image nor the constant echoes from earlier uses nor the altered tenor of the imagery nor the immersion of self in soul, but simply the awe-inspiring assurance with which Arnold handles the image and his eagerness to make it do his bidding. While in the other poems the quest image forms one unbroken tableau from which *exempla* are dependent like captions from cartoons, here the image is, intricately involved, both the fabric and the vision. Arnold seems to feel now that most things are susceptible of statement in terms of this imagery.

The whole poem is now conceived in the image of the quest, and as Arnold's whole effort in the poem is an attempt to discover the truth, he is questing when he approaches the chapel, to strip away its sombre robe of darkness. His father's death is described as a quest for the Master. The life of common men is described as a quest short-circuited by animality and turned into a rat-race. The life of less submissive souls— less submissive to material lures, but equally, if not more so, to the clarion of ego—is depicted as a purposeful, but misguided quest for personal salvation, devil take the hindmost. The lives of the 'noble and great', in whom for the first time Arnold now believes fully, is seen in terms of the quest of the shepherd for the fold, directing his flock towards its haven, with labour probably inestimable, with a sense of duty and a feeling of compassion directing his toil. The present progress, slow, broken, wearisome of mankind is seen to be analogous to the exodus of Israel from Egypt, to be a modern version of the quest of the children of God for the Promised Land. And, in the culminating vision, the race of men are shown, struggling toward the successful accomplishment of the eternal quest for light, and with a faith and an assurance such as Arnold never exhibited in his poetry before, Arnold cheers them on.

In point of form, then, it seems impossible that Arnold could have produced 'Rugby Chapel' before the imagery had, so to speak, served its apprenticeship in the other great spiritual poems. Everywhere in his poetry Arnold's method is to cherish and mature a body of imagery until it is as malleable as the quest image becomes by the time it appears in 'Rugby Chapel', after it has been worked through 'The Scholar-Gipsy', 'Stanzas from the Grande Chartreuse' and 'Thyrsis'. Besides, the calculation with which this imagery is employed in the poem and the manner in which it catches up and restates themes presented by means of it elsewhere demonstrates a determination on Arnold's part to make the links between these poems not merely perceptible but inescapable. In point of substance, it seems quite as unlikely that Arnold could have produced this incisive, almost surgical, analysis of his error, the portrait of the master-philanthropist or the paean to man's future which make this poem so outstanding, at any earlier time. Furthermore, read in this sequence, the great spiritual poems are the record of what is undeniably a continuous spiritual development, culminating in 'Rugby Chapel', incomplete without it and particularly defective without its summary of the process and its attempt to define its tone and mood. . . .

From 'The Road to Rugby Chapel', *University of Toronto Quarterly*, Vol. 34, 1965, pp. 178–96, (188–96).

WALTER E. HOUGHTON

# Empedocles on Etna

It is now twenty years since Sturge Moore remarked that ' "Empedocles" more and more appears the most considerable poem of a
comparable length by a Victorian'.[1] But if this is so, as I think it is,
there is little evidence of its being generally recognized. Indeed, one
might rather say that whatever its comparative value, no other Victorian
poem of such demonstrable stature has been so neglected. And this
despite two obvious attractions: its importance for the understanding of
Arnold and his poetic life—death, rather—and its expression, especially
in Act II, of strains of thought and feeling which are strikingly modern,
Nevertheless, the few pages in Tinker and Lowry's *Commentary*,
devoted largely to sources, and Bonnerot's rambling introduction to his
French translation are the only available materials of any scope.[2]

## I

The subject of the poem is a man named Empedocles; its meaning, the
picture of his character and state of mind on a morning in middle age
when he leaps to his death. In Act I, scene i, Pausanias and Callicles
refer to his earlier career as statesman, doctor, philosopher and poet,
and discuss his present despondency. After that Empedocles himself
holds the centre of the stage for the rest of the poem, conversing a little
with Pausanias, listening occasionally to the songs of Callicles, but for
the most part expounding his philosophy of life, analyzing his depression,
and explaining his desire for death. As this suggests, 'Empedocles on
Etna' is not a philosophical poem. It is a personal poem, a confession,
a 'dialogue of the mind with itself'.

Who is Empedocles? He is not the Sicilian philosopher who lived in

[1] Matthew Arnold', *Essays and Studies of the English Association*, Vol. 24, 1938,
p. 21. Cf. Kenneth Allott, *Matthew Arnold*, London, 1955, p. 25: 'When the
devil's advocate has done his worst, "Empedocles on Etna" remains perhaps the
best long poem by a Victorian'.

[2] C. B. Tinker and H. F. Lowry, *The Poetry of Matthew Arnold. A Com-
mentary*, London, 1940, pp. 286–303; Louis Bonnerot, *Matthew Arnold,
'Empédocle sur L'Etna' ('Empedocles on Etna')*, Etude Critique et Traduction,
Paris, 1947, hereafter referred to as 'Bonnerot, Translation'. Other discussions
or scattered remarks to take account of may be found in: Douglas Bush,
*Mythology and the Romantic Tradition in English Poetry*, Cambridge, 1937, pp.
253–8; Lionel Trilling, *Matthew Arnold*, New York, 1939; reprinted, 1949;
Louis Bonnerot, *Matthew Arnold, Poète* Paris, 1947; J. D. Jump, *Matthew
Arnold*, London, 1955, pp. 82–96, In various ways I am indebted to a discussion
about the poem which I had with Professor Robert Stange of the University of
Minnesota.

the fifth century B.C. No one can read the existing Fragments, or what is known of his life and times, and imagine that Arnold was trying to recreate the man or his thought or his environment. He left out his democratic politics; altered his temperament by omitting the arrogance and substituting a new motivation for the suicide; adopted the idea of a return at death either to the elements or to a new life on earth, but changed its nature and purpose; barely touched on the notion of Love versus Strife, which is the central idea of Empedocles' cosmology; and greatly intensified the note of scepticism and melancholy.[3] All in all, it is fair to say that the pre-Socratic philosopher would never have recognized his mind or his character in the protagonist of the poem.

On the other hand, is Empedocles Arnold himself? In the summer of 1849 J. C. Shairp wrote to Clough that their friend Matt 'was working at an "Empedocles"—which seemed to be not much about the man who leapt in the crater—but his name and outward circumstances are used for the drapery of his own thoughts' (*Commentary*, p. 287). That promising notion of identifying the hero with the poet was indignantly repudiated by Arnold in a letter of 1867 to Henry Dunn: 'You . . . appear to assume that I merely use Empedocles and Obermann as mouthpieces through which to vent my own opinions. This is not so'. And he went on to say that when he was reading the early Greek philosophers fifteen years ago, he had been so impressed by Empedocles he had 'desired to gather up and draw out as a whole the hints which his remains offered' (*Commentary*, pp. 287–8). If that *was* his desire fifteen years ago, he did not carry it out. More likely it was what he now wished he *had* desired, now in 1867, long after he had turned away from the mood of 'Empedocles'—or suppressed it—and was hailing the dawn of a new age of morality touched with emotion in which the son of Dr Arnold was to play a constructive role. This is clearly seen in the concluding stanzas, spoken in propria persona, of 'Obermann Once More', which appeared in the *New Poems*, issued in the same year as the letter to Dunn, and which pointed forward to *Literature and Dogma* and the other formulations of Arnold's version of Christianity. Under those circumstances he was almost forced to dissociate himself, so far as he honestly could, from his 'Empedocles' (here—unfortunately from this point of view—reprinted for the first time since 1852).[4] His letter to

[3] Cf. Bonnerot, Translation, pp. 30–4. He gives a list of occasional verbal echoes on pp. 18–23. For a translation of the Fragments of Empedocles with a critical commentary, see John Burnet, *Early Greek Philosophy*, 4th ed., London, 1930, pp. 197–250.

[4] The letter to his mother of 16 November 1867, in *The Letters of Matthew Arnold*, ed. G. W. E. Russell, 2 vols., London, 1901, Vol. I, pp. 436–7, amounts almost to proof of this interpretation. There Arnold speaks of Swinburne's praise of the 1867 volume (see n.34 below) having inclined the religious world to look out in his writings 'for a crusade against religion', and goes on to say that certain periodicals 'fix on the speeches of Empedocles and Overmann, and calmly say, dropping all mention of the real speakers, "Mr. Arnold here professes his Pantheism", or "Mr. Arnold here disowns Christianity". ' But this will not, he hopes, do as much harm as it would have done two years before.

Dunn continued: 'I have now, and no doubt had still more then, a sympathy with the figure Empedocles presents to the imagination; but neither then nor now would my creed, if I wished or were able to draw it out in black and white, be by any means identical with that contained in the preachment of Empedocles'. For Arnold to confess his sympathy even now, and to say only that his own creed was not *identical* with Empedocles', comes very close to admitting the connection he had just denied.

And yet, if Empedocles is not Empedocles, neither is he Arnold. As the last quotation implies, he is the figure which the historical character presented to Arnold's imagination in 1849. Or more exactly, he is the result of a process in which the imagination dissolved, diffused, and dissipated in order to recreate: in order, let us say, to recreate the historical character in the image of a nineteenth-century intellectual. When *Empedocles on Etna and Other Poems* came out in 1852, Arnold wrote to Clough: 'But woe was upon me if I analysed not my situation: and Werter, René, and such like, none of them analyse the modern situation in its true *blankness* and *barrenness* . . .'[5] A year later, in the Preface to his third volume, he said explicitly:

> I intended to delineate the feelings of one of the last of the Greek religious philosophers, one of the family of Orpheus and Musaeus, having survived his fellows, living on into a time when the habits of Greek thought and feeling had begun fast to change, character to dwindle, the influence of Sophists to prevail. Into the feelings of a man so situated there entered much that we are accustomed to consider as exclusively modern; how much, the fragments of Empedocles himself which remain to us are sufficient at least to indicate. What those who are familiar only with the great monuments of early Greek genius suppose to be its exclusive characteristics, have disappeared; the calm, the cheerfulness, the disinterested objectivity have disappeared: the dialogue of the mind with itself has commenced; modern problems have presented themselves; we hear already the doubts, we witness the discouragement, of Hamlet and of Faust.[6]

As a scholarly statement, that is open to considerable question. But as an indication of how Arnold's imagination was modifying the image of Empedocles by the 'predominant passion' of Hamlet and Faust—and Werther and René, let alone Manfred and Teufelsdröckh, Senancour and Lélia and Clough, and Arnold himself—it tells the precise truth.[7]

---

[5] *The Letters of Matthew Arnold to Arthur Hugh Clough*, ed. H. F. Lowry, London, 1932, p. 126.

[6] *The Poetical Works of Matthew Arnold*, ed. C. B. Tinker and H. F. Lowry, London, 1950, p. xvii. All quotations from the poem or the 1853 Preface are from this edition.

[7] Mrs. Iris E. Sells, *Matthew Arnold and France*, Cambridge, 1935, Ch. 10, shows that a large number of passages in Arnold's poem express sentiments that are also found in Senancour's *Obermann*.

That is why, even though the poem is the portrayal of a character named Empedocles and not an autobiography, the essays and poems and letters of Matthew Arnold—especially the Oxford lecture 'On the Modern Element in Literature'—are a valid commentary and more useful than the Fragments of the philosopher.

II

In his opening lecture at Oxford, given five years after the publication of his major poem, Arnold began by saying that an 'intellectual deliverance' was the peculiar demand of those ages and those nations that could be called modern.

> The demand arises, because our present age has around it a copious and complex present, and behind it a copious and complex past; it arises, because the present age exhibits to the individual man who contemplates it the spectacle of a vast multitude of facts awaiting and inviting his comprehension. The deliverance consists in man's comprehension of this present and past. . . . He who has found that point of view, he who adequately comprehends this spectacle, has risen to the comprehension of his age: he who communicates that point of view to his age, he who interprets to it that spectacle, is one of his age's intellectual deliverers.

The deliverance consists in more than mere understanding; or, to put it more accurately, the understanding includes adjustment. The great writer enables us 'to know how we ourselves stand, that we may correct our mistakes and achieve our deliverance'.[8]

This is the role in which Empedocles is cast and which he plays in Act I. Arnold's own outline for the poem makes this clear:

> He is a philosopher.
>
> He has not the religious consolation of other men, facile because adapted to their weaknesses, or because shared by all around and changing [charging?] the atmosphere they breathe.
>
> He sees things as they are—the world as it is—God as he is: in their stern simplicity.
>
> The sight is a severe and mind-tasking one: to know the mysteries which are communicated to others by fragments, in parables.
>
> But he started towards it in hope: his first glimpses of it filled him with joy: he had friends who shared his hope & joy & communicated to him theirs: even now he does not deny that the sight is capable of affording rapture & the purest peace.
>
> But his friends are dead: the world is all against him, & incredulous of the truth.                                   (*Commentary*, p. 291)

---

[8] *Essays by Matthew Arnold*, London, 1914, pp. 455–7. The didactic function is underscored later on, p. 472, when Arnold says that Horace 'is not interpretative and fortifying'. At the very start, p. 455, he mentions a 'moral deliverance'— from pride, sloth, anger, selfishness—but that does not bear on 'Empedocles'.

The 'truth' is in the so-called sermon preached by Empedocles to Pausanias, where the older, religious view of man is seen displaced by the 'scientific' picture of a universe devoid of moral or spiritual values; and where a new ethic, mainly Stoic, is brought forward in keeping with the new outlook. When Empedocles concludes,

> I say: Fear not! Life still
> Leaves human effort scope.
> But, since life teems with ill,
> Nurse no extravagant hope;
> Because thou must not dream, thou need'st not then despair!
>
> (I, ii, 422–6)

Pausanias—and the nineteenth-century reader—has received his deliverance.

Further on in the Oxford lecture Arnold turns from Greek to Roman literature, and specifically to 'a great poet, a great philospher, Lucretius'. He sees him as complementary to the figure of Thucydides, whom he has just presented as an intellectual deliverer similar to 'a thoughtful philosophic man of our own days' like Burke or Niebuhr.[9] He then continues: 'Let me call attention to the exhibition in Lucretius of a modern *feeling* not less remarkable than the modern *thought* in Thucydides. The predominance of thought, of reflection, in modern epochs . . . has produced a state of feeling unknown to less enlightened but perhaps healthier epochs—the feeling of depression, the feeling of *ennui*. Depression and *ennui*; these are the characteristics stamped on how many of the representative works of modern times! they are also the characteristics stamped on the poem of Lucretius'. And also stamped on Arnold's poem, mainly on Act II, where these characteristics are analyzed into their various components, are a sense of frustration, restlessness, and futility; deep fatigue of body and spirit; isolation and loneliness, cosmic and social; and therefore also nostalgia for an earlier age of peace and faith and moral integrity, and for an earlier time in his own life of joyous intercourse with man and nature, both lost now forever. Again, the outline of the poem leaves no doubt of it: 'His mind is overtasked by the effort to hold fast so great & severe a truth in solitude: the atmosphere he breathes not being modified by the presence of human life, is too rare for him. . . . His spring and elasticity of mind are gone: he is clouded, oppressed, dispirited, without hope & energy' (*Commentary*, pp. 291–2). In the character of Empedocles and in the two acts of the play, respectively, Arnold saw the possibility of portraying both 'modern thought' and 'modern feeling'. Whether in doing so he achieved a unified work of art is another question, still to be considered.

It was this idea, I think, which dictated the form of the work. Though perhaps never thought of as a play to be produced, 'Empedocles' was certainly a dramatic poem as Arnold defined the term in the same lecture

[9] Pp. 461–2. The quotation that follows is on p. 468. For the influence of Lucretius on the poem, see *Commentary*, pp. 292–7.

(*Essays*, p. 470). For the poetic treatment of past events the epic poem, he said, was 'a less vital form than the dramatic form'. In an epic the poet has to represent not only the thought and passion of man, but also 'the forms of outward life, the fashion of manners, the aspects of nature, that which is local or transient'. This can never be done effectively, he suggested, when a poet has to reconstruct an age he knows only through books. But since 'the dramatic form exhibits, above all, *the actions of man as strictly determined by his thoughts and feelings*' (precisely the focus of Arnold's poem) and need not bother with historical environment (patently omitted from Arnold's poem), it can exhibit what is always accessible, intelligible, and interesting.

Since Empedocles' thought, developed in Act I, is not for him a deliverance, it is the modern feeling of ennui that dominates his mind through Act II. This development is made explicit at once in the opening speech:

> Pausanias is far hence, and that is well,
> For I must henceforth speak no more with man.
> He hath his lesson too, and that debt's paid;
> And the good, learned, friendly, quiet man
> May bravelier front his life, and in himself
> Find henceforth energy and heart. But I—
> The weary man, the banish'd citizen,
> Whose banishment is not his greatest ill,
> Whose weariness no energy can reach,
> And for whose hurt courage is not the cure—
> What should I do with life and living more?    (5–15)

For him, then, the courage he has given Pausanias[10] to live without religious illusion, by cultivating a Stoic self-dependence and an Epicurean enjoyment of nature and friendship, is impossible. For him there is only the alternative of suicide.

It might be thought that this constitutes an implied rejection of the philosophy preached in Act I. Arnold himself said as much in the letter to Henry Dunn: 'No critic appears to remark that if Empedocles throws himself into Etna his creed can hardly be meant to be one to live by. If the creed of Empedocles were, as exhibited in my poem, a satisfying one, he ought to have lived after delivering himself of it, not died' (*Commentary*, p. 288). But the date, we remember, is 1867 when Arnold was intent upon preaching his new Christianity. Years earlier, surely, he meant—at any rate, he presented—the creed of Empedocles as one to live by, even though not one sufficient to cure those who suffer, like Empedocles, from profound depression. He said so himself at the time,

---

[10] The summary advice is at I, ii, 397–426. Pausanias was a disciple of Empedocles to whom one of the poems, the *Purifications*, was dedicated: see Burnet, p. 201, n. 1. He is the Horatio of the poem, the friendly man of good will (cf. II, 8, in the quotation just given) who lacks the distinction of intelligence and imagination possessed by the protagonist: see, for illustration, the dialogue at I, ii, 19–38.

G

in the outline of the poem, when he described Empedocles as being
overtasked by trying to hold fast to 'so great & severe a truth', and when
he added: 'He perceives still the truth of the truth [sic], but cannot be
transported and rapturously agitated by his [its?] grandeur: his spring
and elasticity of mind are gone: he is clouded, oppressed, dispirited,
without hope & energy' (*Commentary*, pp. 291–2). Both the belief and
the incapacity to find it sustaining are plainly expressed in the opening
speech. So long as we read 'Empedocles' as a psychological and not a
philosophical poem, there is no problem. Men believe in creeds they
cannot live by.

The next lines continue the 'prologue' to Act II:

> No, thou art come too late, Empedocles!
> And the world hath the day, and must break thee,
> Not thou the world. With men thou canst not live,
> Their thoughts, their ways, their wishes, are not thine:
> And being lonely thou art miserable,
> For something has impair'd thy spirit's strength,
> And dried its self-sufficing fount of joy.          (16–22)

After that description of the two areas of his ennui, the next two lines
are pivotal: 'Thou canst not live with men nor with thyself— / O sage!
O sage! — Take then the one way left', after which the passage ends
(25–36) by referring to the two immediate motivations for the suicide.
I call this a 'prologue' because all of Act II is here implicit. Why
Empedocles cannot live either with men in society or with himself in
solitude is the subject of lines 37–330; why he now, at this moment,
decides to take his life points forward to lines 331–416. At the end of the
play, the chorus-like song of Callicles (417–69) may be viewed as an
'epilogue'.

The first theme—alienation from society—is introduced by Callicles'
song about Typho, son of Gaea the earth, the 'Titan king' of an older
order who rebelled against the new Olympian gods. He was defeated
by Zeus only because of a treacherous act of the Destinies,[11] and
confined in Tartarus under Etna where his 'fierce soul' and 'tortured
heart' still writhe in pain. The analogies with Empedocles in character
and temper and in circumstance (he too pushed aside by a younger
generation and now planning to leap into the same crater) are patent.
He himself seizes on the parallel with his own banishment:

> He fables, yet speaks truth!
> The brave, impetuous heart yields everywhere
> To the subtle, contriving head;
> Great qualities are trodden down,
> And littleness united
> Is become invincible. . . .

---

[11] The treachery (line 54) is underscored by Arnold's note on p. 500.

> Over all the world
> What suffering is there not seen
> Of plainness oppress'd by cunning,
> As the well-counsell'd Zeus oppress'd
> That self-helping son of earth!
> What anguish of greatness,
> Rail'd and hunted from the world,
> Because its simplicity rebukes
> This envious, miserable age!
>
> I am weary of it.                    (89–94; 99–108)

Sufficiently weary, indeed, to discard the symbols of civic power he had once held, his golden circlet and purple robe.[12]

The next section (121–234) follows the same pattern, a song of Callicles' and the train of thought it aroused, but here with a shift of focus to the second theme. After the story of scornful Apollo's cruelty to the fawn Marsyas, Empedocles takes off his laurel bough and places it beside the civic crown and purple robe. Poetry too is renounced because he cannot endure the solitude where the poet must abide: he feels too much alone, too far from life, above all, too much thrown back upon himself, with whom he cannot live—for reasons not yet clear beyond the general state of depression. Then the first theme of Act II reappears in another form. It is not only the hostility of the new society toward greatness but the insidious tendency of social life to stifle the individual self that makes it impossible for Empedocles to live with men:

> Where shall thy votary fly then? back to men?
> But they will gladly welcome him once more,
> And help him to unbend his too tense thought,
> And rid him of the presence of himself,
> And keep their friendly chatter at his ear,
> And haunt him, till the absence from himself,
> That other torment, grow unbearable;         (220–6)

with the result that he will fly to solitude again, and again find its air too keen, and so change back; 'and only death / Can cut his oscillations short, and so / Bring him to poise. There is no other way' (232–234).[13]

---

[12] Behind the passage lies Arnold's distaste for the commercial and democratic character of modern society: see especially 'Rugby Chapel', 145–58, and the opening of 'Milton', *Essays in Criticism, Second Series*. In the year 'Empedocles' was published he wrote to Clough (*Letters to Clough*, p. 122): 'A great career is hardly possible any longer—can hardly now be purchased even by the sacrifice of repose dignity and inward clearness . . . I am more and more convinced that the world tends to become more comfortable for the mass, and more uncomfortable for those of any natural gift or distinction'.

[13] In the Oxford lecture, *Essays*, p. 469, Arnold says of Lucretius: 'There is no peace, no cheerfulness for him either in the world from which he comes, or in the solitude to which he goes'; and illustrates this with a quotation on p. 468 from the *De Rerum Natura*, iii, 1060–1068. Cf. 'Stanzas in Memory of the Author of Obermann', written in the autumn of 1849, 93–6.

'Poise' here means 'rest', but a second meaning comes at once to
Empedocles' consciousness (the ambiguity of words is a causal factor
in all dialogues of the mind with itself) and releases the nostalgia which
has been mounting as he pushed aside each symbol of the past. He now
recalls an earlier time when he was sufficiently poised between the life
of thought in solitude and the life of friendly intercourse in society to
enjoy them both. And they *could* be enjoyed because then he was poised
in still another sense: he possessed a balanced or unified sensibility able
to digest every kind of experience whether intellectual or social. These
related ideas merge into one another as they would in such a 'thinking
aloud', their edges overlapping. 'Then', he says, speaking of himself and
his fellow-philosopher Parmenides,

                              then neither thought
Nor outward things were closed and dead to us;
But we received the shock of mighty thoughts
On simple minds with a pure natural joy;
And if the sacred load oppress'd our brain,
We had the power to feel the pressure eased,
The brow unbound, the thoughts flow free again,
In the delightful commerce of the world,.
We had not lost our balance then, nor grown
Thought's slaves, and dead to every natural joy.      (240–9)

He had not yet, that is, become a philosopher enslaved to abstract specu-
lation and so cut off from the natural life of man which he goes on to
describe in the next lines. This incipient suggestion of the death of a
poet is soon to be developed.

But first he returns to the theme of social dislocation, set in the same
context of nostalgia:

But he, whose youth fell on a different world
From that on which his exiled age is thrown—
Whose mind was fed on other food, was train'd
By other rules than are in vogue to-day—
Whose habit of thought is fix'd, who will not change,
But, in a world he loves not, must subsist
In ceaseless opposition, be the guard
Of his own breast, fetter'd to what he guards,
That the world win no mastery over him—
Who has no friend, no fellow left, not one; . . .
Joy and the outward world must die to him,
As they are dead to me.            (262–71, 274–5)

The note of fear is unmistakable. Here the world threatens to do more
than suppress the individual self by immersing it in social life. It may
even drag the soul (33), formed in an earlier age of moral integrity, into
an environment where it will be debased. The contrast of two ages is

then given a further dimension as Empedocles looks up at the stars:

> You, too, once lived;
> You, too, moved joyfully
> Among august companions
> In an older world, peopled by Gods,
> In a mightier order,
> The radiant, rejoicing, intelligent Sons of Heaven.
> But now, ye kindle
> Your lonely, cold-shining lights,
> Unwilling lingerers
> In the heavenly wilderness,
> For a younger, ignoble world; . . .
> Without friend and without home;
> Weary like us, though not
> Weary with our weariness.　(282–92; 298–300)

The younger world is not only ignoble, it is also atheist. Perhaps ignoble *because* atheist. And since it is without character or faith, it leaves those whose youth fell on a different world in social as well as cosmic isolation: without friend or home in society or the universe.[14]

But in one crucial respect Empedocles finds a difference between the stars and himself. It is the same difference so keenly felt, a few moments before, between the vibrant days of his youth and his present state of mind. The stars are alive; he alone is dead to life and joy. After a long silence, he continues:

> Oh, that I could glow like this mountain!
> Oh, that my heart bounded with the swell of the sea!
> Oh, that my soul were full of light as the stars!
> Oh, that it brooded over the world like the air!
>
> But no, this heart will glow no more; thou art
> A living man no more, Empedocles!
> Nothing but a devouring flame of thought—
> But a naked, eternally restless mind!　　　(323–30)

So far as the poem defines it, this is the 'something' that has impaired his 'spirit's strength and dried its self-sufficing fount of joy' (21–2). This is to grow 'thought's slaves' and therefore incapable of responding at all, let alone joyfully, to the life of man and nature. It is to become not only a restless mind, always seeking an elusive truth (the elation of lines 238–9 has long since disappeared before repeated failure), but also a naked mind, unfleshed by the senses and the feelings, an intellectual skeleton. That was Coleridge's tragedy too, when by abstruse research he stole from his own nature all the natural man—'Till that

---

[14] Comparison may be made with 'Stanzas from the Grande Chartreuse', especially the last stanzas, 169–210, and with 'The Youth of Nature', 28–35.

which suits a part infects the whole, / And now is almost grown the habit of my soul'—with the same painful loss of joy and 'aliveness' and creative power, and the same profound dejection of spirit.[15]

### III

If it is true that the subject of the poem is the man Empedocles and its meaning his frame of mind on the day of the action, the protagonist of Act II should also be the protagonist of Act I. This is clearly the case. The sermon is preached by Empedocles the philosopher, whose 'modern thought' is intended as a deliverance. But his 'modern feeling' runs through the passage too. We hear the voice of the man who found society as intolerable as he found himself.

> What? hate, and awe, and shame
> Fill thee to see our time;
> Thou feelest thy soul's frame
> Shaken and out of chime?
> What? life and chance go hard with thee too, as with us;
>
> Thy citizens, 'tis said,
> Envy thee and oppress,
> Thy goodness no men aid,
> All strive to make it less;
> Tyranny, pride, and lust, fill Sicily's abodes; . . .
>
> The sophist sneers: Fool, take
> Thy pleasure, right or wrong.
> The pious wail: Forsake
> A world these sophists throng.          (112–21, 132–5)

Nor is that all. We also feel, he adds, 'the burden of our selves.' This dual source of Empedocles' depression has already been announced in the previous scene. There Pausanias explains that now he 'lives a lonely man in triple gloom,'

> since all
> Clouds and grows daily worse in Sicily,
> Since broils tear us in twain, since this new swarm

---

[15] 'Dejection: An Ode', especially stanza vi. In the year after 'Empedocles', Arnold was crying out to Clough, apropos of his own poetry (*Letters to Clough*, p. 136, dated 1 May 1853): 'I feel immensely—more and more clearly—what I *want*—what I have (I believe) lost and choked by my treatment of myself and the studies to which I have addicted myself'. The living man with the integrated sensibility of a poet had been sacrificed to make a 'pure' intellectual. 'I am past thirty, and three parts iced over', he wrote a little earlier (p. 128, dated 12 February 1853), '—and my pen, it seems to me, is even stiffer and more cramped than my feeling'. It should be recalled that in a passage from the Oxford lecture quoted above, p. 88, Arnold traced the modern feeling of depression to 'the predominance of thought, of reflection, in modern epochs'.

Of sophists has got empire in our schools
Where he was paramount, since he is banish'd.      (119–23)

Callicles has a different explanation:

'Tis not the times, 'tis not the sophists vex him;
There is some root of suffering in himself,
Some secret and unfollow'd vein of woe,
Which makes the time look black and sad to him.      (150–3)

If this is so, the black look of the times is nonetheless depressing, as we know from Act II. But the root, no doubt, is the burden of himself.[16]

For one thing, the burden of age. The man who is later to speak the great lament for lost youth—loss of friends, of sensitivity, of joy— speaks here in warning of its brevity:

Our youthful blood
Claims rapture as its right;
The world, a rolling flood
Of newness and delight,
Draws in the enamour'd gazer to its shining breast;

Pleasure, to our hot grasp,
Gives flowers after flowers;
With passionate warmth we clasp
Hand after hand in ours;
Now do we soon perceive how fast our youth is spent.

At once our eyes grow clear!
We see, in blank dismay,
Year posting after year,
Sense after sense decay;
Our shivering heart is mined by secret discontent.      (352–66)

Here the loss of youth is not linked with the loss of poetic sensibility but is connected, by contiguity at any rate, with the other side of the same coin, the 'eternally restless mind'. For the Empedocles of Act I, despite his forceful preaching, is the uneasy intellectual, frustrated of ultimate solutions, struggling in vain to catch up with an ever-increasing body of new knowledge:

But still, as we proceed
The mass swells more and more
Of volumes yet to read,

---

[16] Cf. Arnold's letter of 23 September 1849 (*Letters to Clough*, p. 111): 'These are damned times—everything is against one—the height to which knowledge is come, the spread of luxury, our physical enervation, the absence of great *natures*, the unavoidable contact with millions of small ones, newspapers, cities, light profligate friends . . . our own selves, and the sickening consciousness of our difficulties'.

Of secrets yet to explore.
Our hair grows grey, our eyes are dimm'd, our heart is tamed.[17]

(332–6)

Though metaphysical truth is unattainable, the mind of man can at least devise a way of life, an ethic to live by in a universe from which God and immortality have vanished; and *will* devise it if the man is an Empedocles with a painful awareness of ennui and a recognition, therefore, of the desperate need to provide the Pausaniases of the world, 'Who look on life with eyes / Estranged, like mine, and sad', with something by which they can 'bravelier' front their existence.

But if the same man is the protagonist of the whole play, the impression we get of him in Act I is distinctly different. The tone of his long speech is formal and impersonal, strikingly so when compared with the soliloquy of Act II. The speaker is effaced by the stiff pattern of the stanza: lines 1–4 are trimeter, riming *abab*, and the fifth hexameter, riming with the end line of the next stanza. It is impossible to cast a dramatic speech in such a form. But Arnold had no such intention. He wanted to suppress the personality in order to emphasize the thought. The stage direction, 'Empedocles speaks, accompanying himself in a solemn manner on his harp', indicates at once that the speech is to be in recitative. Such a radical separation of the philosopher from the man, not in ideas and attitudes, where the similarities have been noticed, but in manner and feeling, was a brilliant notion, valid artistically and entirely consonant with classical taste and the expected practice of a Greek thinker. But its success depends on the reader. The lines must not be spoken dramatically, but almost chanted in slow measured phrasing.

Another difference in the Empedocles of the two acts is connected with the profound difference in setting. Act I takes place at morning on the wooded slopes of Etna. As the play opens, a single figure is seen, 'alone, resting on a rock by the path'. It is Callicles.

The mules, I think, will not be here this hour;
They feel the cool wet turf under their feet
By the stream-side, after the dusty lanes
In which they have toil'd all night from Catana,
And scarcely will they budge a yard. O Pan,
How gracious is the mountain at this hour![18]          (1–6)

---

[17] See the whole passage, 317–46, and earlier in the speech, 77–96 and 137–41. Again the shadow of Arnold stands behind his hero. 'Yes', he writes to Clough in 1853 (it is the letter in which he speaks of being 'three parts iced over', p. 130) '—*congestion of the brain* is what we suffer from—I always feel it and say it—and cry for air like my own Empedocles'. Also of the letter quoted in the previous note.

[18] The contrast between the cool beauty and 'purity' of nature and the hot, dusty town is reiterated below at 100–4.

This natural setting, combined with the songs of Callicles, has a bearing
on the action. After the opening description, he continues:

> What mortal could be sick or sorry here?
> I know not in what mind Empedocles,
> Whose mules I follow'd, may be coming up,
> But if, as most men say, he is half mad
> With exile, and with brooding on his wrongs,
> Pausanias, his sage friend, who mounts with him,
> Could scarce have lighted on a lovelier cure.     (20–6)

And presently he urges Pausanias to 'lead him through the lovely
mountain-paths, / And keep his mind from preying on itself' (156–7).
This is equally the function of the young poet, urged in his turn by
Pausanias to 'relax his settled gloom' by playing 'thy noblest strains'.
The first song, therefore, begins with a lovely description of the 'high,
well-water'd dells on Etna', beyond which lies the bare summit, not yet
in view. The second, which has been called a 'green thought in a green
shade',[19] pictures the escape of Cadmus and Harmonia in old age, far,
far from the calamities at Thebes (the parallel calamities at Agrigentum
are in one's mind) to where

> The Adriatic breaks in a warm bay
> Among the green Illyrian hills; and there
> The sunshine in the happy glens is fair,
> And by the sea, and in the brakes.     (428–31)

It is not surprising that as Empedocles listened, 'his brow lighten'd as
the music rose' (483). For him, as for his creator, there were two possible refuges from ennui and depression: a Stoic philosophy and 'the
cool flowery lap of earth'.[20]
But though both can lessen his gloom momentarily, they cannot
exorcise it. The first act closes in symbolic action. As Empedocles 'de-
parts on his way up the mountain', Pausanias, instructed in saving
wisdom, descends, calling to Callicles, whom he has just glimpsed
'through the chestnuts far below . . . down at the stream', to continue
playing. Then at once—and in dramatic contrast also with the opening
of the first act—

### ACT II

*Evening. The summit of Etna.*

#### EMPEDOCLES

Alone!—
On this charr'd, blacken'd, melancholy waste,

---

[19] By Douglas Bush, with an assist from Andrew Marvell.
[20] 'Memorial Verses, 1850', 49. For this refuge, the *locus classicus* is 'The
Scholar-Gipsy'.

Crown'd by the awful peak, Etna's great mouth.
Round which the sullen vapour rolls—alone!

### IV

The suicide is a problem. A number of critics have supposed that after
Act I Empedocles changed his mind 'without sufficient cause assigned',
and on a 'sudden impulse' decided to end his life.[21] Since nothing in the
text supports this theory, it can only rest on the ingenuous assumption
that no man who preached a philosophy to live by could be meditating
his own death. The fact is that before the end of Act I and shortly after
the sermon closes, suicide—and even the notion of probationary return
after death, which he dwells on later in Act II—are plainly in his mind
(I, ii, 471–7). But I see no reason to suppose that that has not been so
all along, though the *final moment* of action may, and does, depend on
a sudden impulse.

Other critics have found the suicide insufficiently motivated (trials
like these are not greater than men can bear!) or else the entirely natural
result of a radical neurosis.[22] In both cases the depression is viewed as
the cause of the death. It is certainly the *sine qua non*, but it is not the
direct or immediate cause. If it were, Empedocles would die in an access
of despair and not, as he does, in a strange mood of exaltation, even of
triumph. Again, Arnold's outline of the poem is our best guide: 'Before
he becomes the victim of depression & overtension of mind, to the utter
deadness to joy, grandeur, spirit, and animated life, he desires to die;
to be reunited with the universe, before by exaggerating his human side
he has become utterly estranged from it' (*Commentary*, p. 292). It is
important to notice that there are two 'before's', bearing respectively
on continued existence here and on existence after death. Empedocles
desires to die before his soul is contaminated by 'a younger, ignoble
world', and his sensibility so dominated by 'thought' that he is 'dead to
life and joy'; and to die before, by exaggerating his intellectual faculty,
he cannot be reunited to nature at death and therefore, as the poem
shows, will have to relive the same unbalanced, estranging life of the
intellect.[23] This is not the whole story—death is also given a strong
emotional appeal—but those reasons, testifying as they do to the resolve
to protect all that is finest in his nature from destruction, give the suicide
its note of moral victory.

[21] R. H Hutton, 'The Poetry of Matthew Arnold', *Literary Essays*, London,
1892 p. 319; A. H. Clough, 'Review of Some Poems by Alexander Smith and
Matthew Arnold', *Prose Remains* London, 1888, p. 362.

[22] Hutton, and J. A. Froude, 'Arnold's Poems', *Westminster Review*, Vol. 61,
1854, p. 154, for the first; Bonnerot, Translation, p. 54, for the second. Froude's
anonymous essay is reprinted in various editions of his *Short Studies on Great
Subjects*.

[23] In the quotation just given, Arnold calls the intellect 'his human side'
because reason differentiates man from the animals, and because for Empedocles it exists only in human life and has no element from which it came and
to which it can return.

This account of the matter lies behind the conclusion of what I have called the 'prologue' to Act II:

> O sage! O sage!—Take then the one way left;
> And turn thee to the elements, thy friends,
> Thy well-tried friends, thy willing ministers,
> And say: Ye helpers, hear Empedocles,
> Who asks this final service at your hands!    (24–8)

That is to say, who asks it *now* before the hypertrophy of the mind will make it impossible. And

> Before the sophist-brood hath overlaid
> The last spark of man's consciousness with words—
> Ere quite the being of man, ere quite the world
> Be disarray'd of their divinity—
> Before the soul lose all her solemn joys,
> And awe be dead, and hope impossible,
> And the soul's deep eternal night come on—
> Receive me, hide me, quench me, take me home!    (29–36)

In short, he would rather die now than live to see his soul, which had been 'fed on other food' and 'trained by other rules than are in vogue today', infected and destroyed by a new environment that is utterly lacking in moral and spiritual quality.[24]

The latter notion, in keeping with Empedocles' philosophic leanings, is Stoic, Arnold must have known the fine passage of Epictetus on the death of Socrates: by dying, 'he intended to preserve something else, not his poor flesh, but his fidelity, his honourable character'. He would save, not his body, but 'that which is increased and saved by doing what is just, and is impaired and destroyed by doing what is unjust'. He would be useful to men by giving an example of a man's 'dying when we ought to die, and as we ought'.[25] The return to the elements at death is also Stoic doctrine, but that Arnold found directly in the Fragments of Empedocles,[26] where he also found the idea of purgatorial wandering:

> There is an oracle of Necessity, an ancient ordinance of the gods, eternal and sealed fast by broad oaths, that whenever one of the daemons, whose portion is length of days, has sinfully polluted his hands with blood, *or followed strife and forsworn himself*, he must wander thrice ten thousand seasons from the abodes of the blessed, being born throughout the time in all manners of mortal forms,

[24] Cf. II, 262–270, from which the quoted phrases are taken. For this Arnoldian fear of the soul's contamination, see, for example, 'Fragment of Chorus of a "Dejaneira" ', 'Palladium'. and 'The Youth of Man', 112–118.

[25] Epictetus, *Discourses*, IV, i, 161, 164, 168, tr. George Long, New York, 1900, pp. 311–12.

[26] Epictetus, III, xiii, 15, in Long, p. 228, speaks of returning 'to your friends and kinsmen, to the elements'. Cf. II. 24–6, quoted just above. For Empedocles, see Burnet, p. 245.

changing one toilsome path of life for another. For the mighty Air drives him into the Sea, and the Sea spews him forth on the dry Earth; Earth tosses him into the beams of the blazing Sun, and he flings him back to the eddies of Air. One takes him from the other, and all reject him. One of these I now am, an exile and a wanderer from the gods, for that I put my trust in insensate strife.[27]

That is the eschatology which Arnold adapted to his special purpose in the great passage which follows the charge that he has become 'Nothing but a devouring flame of thought— / But a naked, eternally restless mind' (329–30).

'Eternally restless' not only here, he seems to say (we can almost see the mind pivoting on the ambiguity of the adverb), but hereafter too. For he continues:

> To the elements it came from
> Everything will return—
> Our bodies to earth,
> Our blood to water,
> Heat to fire,
> Breath to air.
> They were well born, they will be well entomb'd—
> But mind? . . .                    (331–8)

The ominous question is pushed aside, momentarily, as Empedocles the man associates the philosopher's theory of a 'good' death with the recovery of everything he has lost in the past: life and joy and companionship, and the creative spirit.

> And we might gladly share the fruitful stir
> Down in our mother earth's miraculous womb;
> Well would it be
> With what roll'd of us in the stormy main;
> We might have joy, blent with the all-bathing air,
> Or with the nimble, radiant life of fire.     (339–44)

The suggestion in 'mother' of a return 'home', followed as it is (in the next lines) by the prospect of being forever homeless if death is delayed, merges with the earlier idea of the elements as friends (at lines 25–8) to give death the powerful attraction of ending his isolation and loneliness. But mind?

> But mind, but thought—
> If these have been the master part of us—
> Where will *they* find their parent element?
> What will receive *them* who will call *them* home?
> But we shall still be in them and they in us,
> And we shall be the strangers of the world,

---

[27] Burnet, p. 222, with commentary on p. 250. The italics are mine.

And they will be our lords, as they are now;
And keep us prisoners of our consciousness.
And never let us clasp and feel the All
But through their forms, and modes, and stifling veils.     (345–54)

To know the world only through the forms and modes of the logical
mind is simply to continue the existence he is already leading, cut off,
as by a stifling veil, from direct experience of man and nature, joyless,
as he goes on to say, lifeless, homeless. But the new or second existence
is probationary:[28]

To see if we will poise our life at last,
To see if we will now at last be true
To our own only true, deep-buried selves,
Being one with which we are one with the whole world;
Or whether we will once more fall away
Into some bondage of the flesh or mind,
Some slough of sense, or some fantastic maze
Forged by the imperious lonely thinking-power.     (369–76)

In 'lonely' the two themes of Act II are again linked, as they have been
earlier by nostalgia for the past. Just as he feels estranged from modern
society, so also, having forsworn his true, deep-buried self, the poet with
his unified sensibility, he feels isolated from the world of concrete
reality, living alone in a fantastic maze, imprisoned in the Ivory Tower,
not of Art, but of Thought.

In the lines that follow, his hopeless view of probation is significant
(we shall rally our powers for one last fight, and fail, and be astray
forever) since it drives home the wisdom of dying before 'the human
side' has become so dominant that reunion with nature is impossible.
For though he has charged himself with being a living man no more,
that is not quite the truth—not yet but almost, close enough to say so.
For at this point, after denying he has been a slave of sense, he now
*asks*, 'But slave of thought? . . .' and then continues:

And who can say: I have been always free,
Lived ever in the light of my own soul?—
I cannot; I have lived in wrath and gloom,
Fierce, disputatious, ever at war with man,
Far from my own soul, far from warmth and light.     (392–6)

If he has not quite succumbed to the tyranny of thought, he has been
led into the intellectual strife that goes with it, and has nourished a
belligerent spirit far from love. Still, he can add: 'But I have not grown
easy in these bonds— / But I have not denied what bonds these were'
(397–8). That sense of having been true to his ideals, at least in

---

[28] This seems to be Arnold's idea. In Empedocles the succession of lives not
only involves transmigration through the forms of various plants and animals
(see Burnet, pp. 223–4), but is thought of simply as a punishment.

theory, is then developed more confidently in an assertion of moral
strength:

Yea, I take myself to witness,
That I have loved no darkness,
Sophisticated no truth,
Nursed no delusion,
Allow'd no fear!

    And therefore, O ye elements! I know—
Ye know it too—it hath been granted me
Not to die wholly, not to be all enslaved.
I feel it in this hour. The numbing cloud
Mounts off my soul; I feel it, I breathe free.    (399–408)

The glad realization that he is not yet *wholly* dead, not *all* enslaved to
the mind or to the world (both seem implied, but mainly the former)
brings with it, as tangible confirmation, the very pulse of life. Where
shortly before he had prayed, 'Oh, that I could glow like this mountain',
and had answered wearily, 'But no, this heart will glow no more', he
can now throw off the numbing cloud of despondency and cry out to
the elements, 'My soul glows to meet you'. The very thing he thought
never to experience again sweeps over him, and in the context of the
argument—the wisdom of dying before he sinks once more into a
despondency that must soon give the intellect and the world their
mastery over him, and before he becomes unable to return to his mother
earth and share in her joyful, creative life—provides the immediate
impulse to carry out his resolve. No wonder he plunges into the crater
triumphantly, crying to the elements, 'Receive me, save me!'

V

Why Arnold withdrew the poem in all editions between 1852 and 1867
is not important in itself but only so far as the reasons can help us to reach
a final evaluation. His own explanation, that because the suffering
found 'no vent in action' and the distress was 'unrelieved by incident,
hope, or resistance', the poem did not meet that requirement of poetry,
to 'inspirit and rejoice', will not survive examination.[29] Empedocles'
assertion of his ideals in the face of hostile forces, in society and himself,
and his dramatic recovery of 'life' in the final moments give the relief
of resistance and incident, and are even, in some degree, inspiriting.
Moreover, as Trilling noted, the suffering of the hero can free a reader
from moments of despair by 'naming and ordering his own incoherent
emotions, taking them beyond the special misery of privacy. . . . There
is a *catharsis* of expression, formulation and understanding as well as of
action'.[30]

[29] Preface to the *Poems* of 1853, *Poetical Works*, p. xviii.
[30] *Matthew Arnold*, p. 153.

The truth is that personal more than artistic reasons lay behind the suppression of the poem. In the early fifties Arnold was struggling to master his own morbid depressions. He felt a growing wish 'not to vacillate and be helpless, but to do my duty'; thought that though in the sterile air of the present times 'we deteriorate in spite of our struggles', still, it was our duty to try and 'keep alive our courage and activity'.[31] It is this attitude, none the less genuine for being filial, which mainly dictated the withdrawal of the poem.[32]

Certainly it underlies the argument that bears on the question in his Oxford lecture. After citing Lucretius as an exponent of depression and ennui, which he called 'the disease of the most modern societies', Arnold criticized him for 'perpetually repeating his formula of disenchantment and annihilation', accused him of being 'overstrained, gloom-weighted, morbid', and then concluded: 'He who is morbid is no adequate interpreter of his age'.[33] But that role, the role of intellectual deliverer, was precisely that in which Empedocles had been cast, and which he fulfilled in Act I, only to rob himself of such a claim, on this theory, by turning morbid in Act II. On that line, I think, Arnold persuaded himself that the two acts were not harmonious. But if the subject of the poem is neither modern thought nor modern feeling but a man who expresses both, the play as a whole is perfectly coherent.

A more valid criticism has centred on the long speech of Empedocles in Act I. Though for Swinburne the finest thing in the poem, modern readers have found it 'prosaic' in expression and superficial in philosophy.[34] The latter charge may be dismissed. The passage is not to be judged as a systematic statement, but as philosophical poetry expressing an ethical outlook on human life; and the particular outlook, Stoicism leavened with elements from Epicureanism, is no more dated than it is superficial. It is, in fact, a view widely held today.

[31] *Letters*, Vol. I, p. 48, dated 9 December 1854; *Letters to Clough*, p. 123, dated 7 June 1852. Cf. *Letters*, Vol. I, p. 60, dated April 1856, and *Letters to Clough*, p. 130, dated 12 February 1853.

[32] Essentially the same point is made in another way by Douglas Bush, *Mythology and the Romantic Tradition*, p. 253: 'His reason for withdrawing the poem . . . may not have been the whole truth. Surely a more vital reason was a perception that he had said the opposite of what he believed he ought to have said. For years he had been trying to suppress his emotions in the interest of a higher intellectual and spiritual life, and 'Empedocles' should have been a song of victory; instead it records the failure of the austere ideal his will had imposed upon himself'.

[33] *Essays*, pp. 468–9. Since I have noted so many connections between this essay and 'Empedocles,' I might complete the list by suggesting that I, ii, 102, 131, and 146 seem to be echoes of Arnold's translation of Lucretius on p. 469.

[34] Swinburne's praise is in his 'Matthew Arnold's New Poems', a review of the 1867 volume, *Essays and Studies*, London, 1875, pp. 126 and 133–7. For some modern critics, see Tinker and Lowry, *Commentary*, p. 301; Jump, p. 88; Bonnerot, Translation, p. 75. Bonnerot's criticism of the whole poem, pp. 72–91, is so severe and cranky one wonders why he took the trouble to translate it at all.

But is the view adequately expressed? If 'prosaic' means that the style has no dramatic urgency, the answer has been made: that Arnold never intended the speech to be anything but a philosophic chant. If it means that the medium of verse—stanza form, rhythm, sound, imagery—is not well utilized to express either the argument or its emotional field (valid demands for philosophical poetry), the point is well taken. Some of the writing is incredibly flat:

> We do not what we ought,
> What we ought not, we do,
> And lean upon the thought
> That chance will bring us through;
> But our own acts, for good or ill, are mightier powers.          (237–41)

Not even a harp could give that the quality of poetry. The rhythm is as awkward as the diction is banal. The whole speech, of course, is not written at that level (the first four stanzas and the last six show what Arnold could do), but too much of it is marred by writing that would lose nothing,—would gain, rather—if cast into prose.

It might be argued that though this analysis is right, the judgment is wrong. Could we say, with one Victorian critic, that 'the metallic hollowness of rhetoric, the wintry sententiousness', betray a man 'who strives to make his heart follow the guidance of his intellect?'[35] Anyone determined to commit suicide might well find it difficult to give adequate expression to a creed he could not live by himself, however useful it might be to others. But if, as I have argued, the speech is not dramatic, we can hardly call its limitations a revelation of character. No, the speech remains for me, not a failure by any means, but the one serious flaw in a fine poem. For everywhere else, I think, the form is at least equal, often more than equal, to the demands of a complex content.[36]

Of the conception of Callicles there can only be the highest praise. Indeed, without it the poem would have been seriously impaired: the action too limited, the tone a little monotonous, and the figure—and meaning—of Empedocles less fully realized. To some extent the songs are part of the action. They bring momentary relief in Act I, as we noticed, to Empedocles' gloom. Or they serve as a kind of chorus, perhaps a kind of counterpoint would be more accurate, played off against his train of thought with implied contrast or sympathy, sometimes both. The first song, immediately preceding the sermon, tells of

---

[35] 'The Poetry of Matthew Arnold', *Edinburgh Review*, Vol. 168, 1888, p. 344.
[36] Of the speech at II, 345–90, Jump, p. 93, has said: 'This is Arnold's finest passage of blank verse; and it is a genuinely dramatic speech. The repetitive sequences of harassed and despairing utterances, each one receiving very much the same degree of emphasis as its neighbours, convey insidiously the bewilderment of men driven hither and thither by "thought and mind"; and the larger rhythm which unites the sequences carries us on, unrestingly and dizzily, to the desolate silence which follows the words "And be astray for ever".'

how Chiron instructed young Achilles in the traditional wisdom he had taught his father Peleus, 'in long distant years', of gods and stars and immortality, and how to live like a traditional hero, with action and glory. As his voice dies away, we hear Empedocles beginning to teach Pausanias the wisdom *he* needs, but the first words are of man in 'doubt and fear, who knows not what to believe', and the final words convey a new wisdom to take the place of traditional religion and to enable a modern hero to 'bravelier front' a life without glory. In Act II the songs about Typho and Marsyas are read by Empedocles as fables that yet speak truths, and prompt him to act, by resignation, on the conclusions already in his mind, that he can neither live with men as statesman nor with himself as poet.

But the major role of Callicles is to give concrete form to an ideal at the opposite pole from the figure of Empedocles: that of the young poet with an alert sensibility, dedicated to the broad contemplation of life, and writing—singing with joy—a poetry of elemental experience: the beauty of nature and the cycle of human existence from birth to death. The very first songs, bounding the central speech of Act I, throw into sharp relief the ageing philosopher, thinking aloud, in abstract and declamatory verse, and, when taken together with the songs of Act II, extend the contrast to include 'the calm, the cheerfulness, the disinterested objectivity' of Callicles' art in opposition to Empedocles' dialogue of the mind with itself.[37] At the end, after the great lament for the tyranny of the intellect, the lovely lyric of Callicles about Apollo and the Muses, singing of gods and men on the moonlit slopes of Mount Helicon, is a final affirmation of art as Yeats described it in *The Cutting of the Agate*: 'Art bids us touch and taste and hear and see the world, and shrinks from what Blake calls mathematic form, from every abstract thing, from all that is of the brain only, from all that is not a fountain jetting from the entire hopes, memories, and sensations of the body.'[38] Besides in this way sharpening the central contrast of the poem, the song also serves, like the last lines of 'Sohrab and Rustum', to place the preceding violence within a larger perspective and thus close the play on a note of serenity.

Even now the meaning of the Callicles image is not exhausted. It also represents, for the reader, Empedocles as he once was, and thereby heightens the tragic sense of what he has lost. The fine speech in which he describes the days 'when we were young' is, in effect, a description of Callicles now,

> We had not lost our balance then, nor grown
> Thought's slaves, and dead to every natural joy.
> The smallest thing could give us pleasure then—
> The sports of the country-people,

[37] The 1853 Preface, *Poetical Works*, p. xvii.
[38] From a section of 'Discoveries' called 'The Thinking of the Body', in *Essays*, New York, 1924, p. 362.

H

A flute-note from the woods,
Sunset over the sea;
Seed-time and harvest,
The reapers in the corn,
The vinedresser in his vineyard,
The village-girl at her wheel.     (II, 248–57)

Against that background the last lines of Callicles' song heighten the tragedy of lost potentiality. There Apollo and the Muses sing of

What will be for ever;
What was from of old.

First hymn they the Father
Of all things; and then,
The rest of immortals,
The action of men.

The day in his hotness,
The strife with the palm;
The night in her silence,
The stars in their calm.     (459–68)

That is the broad, elemental experience which Empedocles himself had delighted in before he became 'nothing but a devouring flame of thought'—and a philosopher; while he was still young and 'alive'—and a poet.

Finally, and perhaps most striking, is the range and weight of experience which the poem brings together. In the best of Arnold's work, and especially here, what makes him ultimately a distinguished poet is his content. He stressed it deliberately. He insisted that a poet should strive 'to attain or approach perfection in the region of thought and feeling, and to unite this with perfection of form'.[39] He meant the most basic thought and feeling of man—at any rate, educated man—in the modern world. To read 'Empedocles' is to find reflections and explorations of a large part of our experience: the scepticism of any ultimate truths, the search for some constructive outlook that can give one 'the courage to be', the distaste for a society that seems devoid of moral values, the acute self-consciousness, the sense of isolation and loneliness, the suspicion of 'pure' intellectualism, the desire for a wholeness in which the total personality may be alive and active, above all, perhaps, the nostalgia—though firmly repressed today and rarely mentioned—for a lost world of youth and peace and simplicity. These are things that we know, timeless and contemporary. They touch our lives at a significant depth. That is why, in the last analysis, 'Empedocles

[39] The quotation is from a letter of 6 September 1858, *Letters*, Vol. I, p. 84. He thought that one way in which his own poetry was superior to Tennyson's or Browning's (*Letters*, Vol. II, p. 10, dated 5 June 1869) was its representation of the main movement of mind in his time.

on Etna' is for us the most impressive poem of its length written in the Victorian period.

From 'Arnold's "Empedocles on Etna" ', *Victorian Studies*, Vol. 1, 1958, pp. 311–36. Some footnotes have been omitted and others have been reduced in length.

GEORGE WATSON

# The Age, the Poet, the Criticism

> . . . the method of historical criticism that great and famous power
> in the present day. . . . The advice to study the character of an
> author and the circumstances in which he has lived, in order to
> account to oneself for his work, is excellent. But it is a perilous
> doctrine that from such a study the right understanding of his work
> will 'spontaneously issue'. 'A French Critic [Edmond Schérer] on
> Milton', *Quarterly Review*, January 1877, reprinted in his *Mixed
> Essays*, 1879.)

This quotation from one of the last and best of the critical essays of
Matthew Arnold (1822–88) suggests at once how untypical a Victorian
critic he was, and how proudly he knew it. The 'great and famous power'
of historical criticism, against which no other Victorian critic before the
nineties raised his voice, seemed to him implausible and over-rated
almost before it had established itself. 'The old story of *the man and the
milieu*'—that is how, in the same essay, he dismisses by misquotation
the grandiose theories of Taine concerning 'race, milieu, moment' as
the occasion for creative energy. Each civilized age has its favourite
discipline from which special enlightenment is expected to flow.
Today it is sociology; for Arnold's age it was undeniably history, and
the new techniques of historical research summed up for the heroine of
George Eliot's *Middlemarch* (1871–2) by the dread word 'German'.
The amateur English tradition of Gibbon and Hallam was falling back
before the systematic researches of Niebuhr and Ranke. The techniques
of textual criticism ('the Higher Criticism', as it came impressively to
be called) had invaded the study of the Bible, and with the publication
of seven *Essays and Reviews* in 1860 was shown to have established itself
inside the Church of England. For the President of Mark Rutherford's
nonconformist seminary in the 1850s the word 'German' was 'a term
of reproach suggesting something very awful, although nobody knew
exactly what it was'.[1] Germany led: France followed only a little behind.
A French reviewer confidently wrote as early as 1825 that the absolute
study of texts was already dead in French criticism, and the day of
historical criticism at hand: 'After long considering literature as some-

---

[1] From his autobiographical novel, *The Autobiography of Mark Rutherford*
(1881), ch. 2.

thing invariable and absolute, capable of submitting itself to prearranged forms, criticism now regards it as the variable and changing product of its own society.'

That was written when Arnold was three years old; in France, at least, the battle for history was already won. But England was submitting very fast. G. H. Lewes (1817–78) hailed the new 'scientific' historiography in his articles in the *Westminster Review* in the 1840s as the foundation of a future 'science of man'. Years later, in a lecture delivered at St Andrews University in 1887, Leslie Stephen (1832–1904), whose long, rambling essays in criticism represent something of a triumph for his own relaxed, anglicized version of continental historicism, cautiously admitted that 'the historical method is now in the ascendant', affecting 'not only history in the old sense, but philosophy, political and social theory, and every other branch of inquiry which has to do with the development of living beings'. 'I will not say', he went on, that the study of literature can be 'made truly scientific'. But literature can be 'treated in a scientific spirit'.[2] A year later, Arnold was dead. He had spent a good deal of his energies for thirty years in denying it all.

The spirit of denial in Arnold's criticism is, on the face of it, the most striking thing about it. He is the great gainsayer of English criticism, the most insistent and professional of nonconformists. His characteristic strategy is, like Pope's Atticus, to 'hesitate dislike'. He delights in sapping confidence. But in all this, paradoxically, he is only behaving after the convention of the Victorian intellectual: rude as he is against established literary values, he is no ruder than Carlyle and Ruskin against established society and morality. Iconoclasm is the strongest and deepest of currents among the Victorian intelligentsia. It was they, after all, who conceived the revolutionary doctrines by which the twentieth century lives and dies, and Arnold in his criticism is just such a spirit of contradiction incarnate. The literary values he recommends are those that the poetry of his day was least able to achieve; his cultural values are everything that cultivated opinion in his own day was not. Both are revolutionary alternatives to the *status quo*; for Arnold, like his contemporary Marx, challenged his own world to suicide and rebirth. The urbanity of his manner is not even superficially a conservative gloss; it was a red rag to a bull in a society that suspected urbanity, it sharpened the challenge.

Arnold's defiance of the Victorian tradition of poetry begins in reaction against himself. In 1849 he had startled his friends with a first collection of poems, *The Strayed Reveller*, where the bright young man just down from Oxford revealed himself as a melancholy romantic in love with solitude. Three years later he reissued his poems with the addition of 'Empedocles on Etna', and in 1853 replaced this drama of suicide with the miniature epic 'Sohrab and Rustum', and a preface written during the summer in reply to an anonymous and deprecating

[2] Leslie Stephen, *Men, Books, and Mountains*, edited by S. O. A. Ullmann, Minneapolis, 1956, pp. 19, 25.

review of 'Empedocles'.[3] The preface to the *Poems* of 1853, written at
the age of thirty-one, is the first of Arnold's prose works, and oddly
stiff and graceless when we think of the ironic elegance of his later prose.
'It is far less *precise* than I had intended', he complained in a letter to his
old school-friend Clough. 'How difficult it is to write prose.' For the
remaining thirty-five years of his life he wrote hardly anything else.

Arnold's criticism measures the distance between his ambition as a
poet and his performance. A poet in the tradition of Keats, he seeks in
his prose to extricate himself from a romanticism he both loves and
despises. Nothing, in the history of criticism, is more familiar than the
spectacle of a poet turning in early middle age to justify his achievements
and rationalize his failures, as Dryden had done—or, like Baudelaire
and Eliot, to explore in prose notions for which, as poets, they felt
themselves unready. Arnold's criticism begins in a more hostile spirit,
in self-disgust, and his attack upon the rejected 'Empedocles' in the
1853 preface, upon its extravagant subjectivity and its lack of action,
is not much less than an attack upon the whole of his brief career as a
poet.

The conscientious distaste for his own poetry which is the starting-
point of Arnold's criticism began very early, before he had published
his first volume of verse. 'What a brute you were', he wrote to Clough
in the winter of 1848-9, 'to tell me to read Keats's letters. . . . What
harm he has done in English poetry. As Browning is a man with a
moderate gift passionately desiring movement and fulness, and obtaining but a confused multitudinousness, so Keats, with a very high
gift, is yet also consumed by this desire: and cannot produce the truly
living and moving, as his conscience keeps telling him. They will not be
patient, neither understand that they must begin with an idea of the
world in order not be to prevailed over by the world's multitudinousness: or, if they cannot get that, at least with isolated ideas,' and he
goes on to condemn the influence upon young writers of Keats, Tennyson, 'yes, and those d—d Elizabethan poets generally'.[4] In October 1852,
in a further letter to Clough, he returns to the same point—that the
greatest poets may be the worst influences:

> Keats and Shelley were on a false track when they set themselves to
> reproduce the exuberance of expression, the charm, the richness of
> images, and the felicity, of the Elizabethan poets. Yet critics cannot
> get to learn this, because the Elizabethan poets are our greatest, and
> our canons of poetry are founded on their works. . . . Modern poetry
> can only subsist by its *contents*: by becoming a complete *magister
> vitae* as the poetry of the Ancients did: by including, as theirs did,
> religion with poetry, instead of existing as poetry only, and leaving
> religious wants to be supplied by the Christian religion.

[3] *North British Review*, May 1853.
[4] *Letters of Matthew Arnold to Arthur Hugh Clough*, edited by H. F. Lowry,
Oxford, 1932, pp. 96-7.

The demand that poetry help to fill the spiritual void felt by a faithless age carries us, with surprising suddenness, into the heart of a conviction he spent many years in justifying: that the poet in an open society and in conditions of expanding literacy must, like priests in the age of priests, offer guidance and instruction, and that the language of such poetry 'must be very plain, direct, and severe: and it must not lose itself in parts and episodes and ornamental work, but must press forward to the whole'. No wonder he felt his own poems were worse than useless, a mere addendum to the vicious, or at best irrelevant, Keatsian tradition. 'The Scholar-Gipsy', written in 1852, he confessed to Clough 'at best awakens a pleasing melancholy. But this is not what we want.' What we do want—and the 1853 preface might almost be considered a manifesto, if the savour of Arnold's own sense of failure did not hang so thickly over it—is a flat rejection of the poetry of the romantics and Elizabethans in favour of poems that are 'particular, precise, and firm', dealing with human actions not rooted in one time or place, but which 'most powerfully appeal to the great primary human affections: to those elementary feelings which subsist permanently in the race'. Here, in its grasp of essentials, lay the virtue of the civilization of the Greeks: 'They regarded the whole; we regard the parts.'

The demand is highly reminiscent, and in two ways. It is reminiscent, first, of Coleridge's call, provoked by the 1800 preface, for a new dignity or 'neutrality' of style in contemporary poetry. And secondly, it sounds a little like the defunct seventeenth-century obsession of English poets and critics with the 'heroic poem'; 'Sohrab and Rustum' and 'Balder Dead', indeed, are little epics, as oddly isolated in time as those epigones of English pastoral poetry, 'The Scholar-Gipsy' and 'Thyrsis'. But both echoes are accidental: Arnold nowhere shows any sign of having absorbed Coleridgean aesthetics, and he is evidently conscious only of the classical epic of Homer and Virgil, while remaining noticeably indifferent to such neoclassical epics as *Paradise Lost*. It was part of the price he paid for rejecting the fashionable historicism of his day that he rarely knew who his own intellectual ancestors were.

In 1857, at the age of thirty-five, Arnold was elected to the Chair of Poetry in Oxford, a position of dignity he held for ten years, with the distinction of being the first incumbent to lecture in the English language. But to say that is to create a false impression at once: a brilliant poet and man-about-town, still young and contemptuous of academic pedantry, blowing away the cobwebs of Latin scholarship in a mood of intellectual liberation. To realize how wrong all this is, one only has to turn to his inaugural lecture of 1857, 'On the Modern Element in Literature'.[5] It is a lecture against the modern element in literature, in which Arnold seeks an alliance with the classical dons in his audience against the prevailing tide of middle-class romanticism. Oxford University, he declared in the preface to the first series of *Essays*

[5] *Macmillan's Magazine*, February 1869, posthumously collected in the so-called *Essays in Criticism: Third Series*, Boston, 1910.

*in Criticism* (1865), 'is generous, and the cause in which I fight is, after all, hers'. This is the voice not of modernity and liberation, but of neo-conservatism, of the candidate for Establishment honours. Arnold might almost be angling for a knighthood. It is true, of course, that the projected alliance between Arnold's New Hellenism and the Old was never effected, and involved too many incongruities ever to be effected; and Arnold may have felt a little ashamed of his Inaugural, with its measured warnings against romantic modernity in favour of ancient classical severity. He did not collect it. Indeed, the first three years of his ensuing Oxford lectures are largely lost (1857–60), and he reappears only in 1860–1, when he delivered three lectures *On Translating Homer* (1861), an attempt to define more closely the qualities of the 'excellent action' of the 1853 preface by means of a summary of the Homeric qualities that any English translator must achieve—rapidity of action, plainness of language, plainness of thought, and nobility—involving himself in controversy with F. W. Newman, whose own version of the *Iliad* (1856) provided Arnold with his whipping-boy. Shortly after, from 1862, he began to publish a series of articles on single authors, which he collected in 1865 under the title of *Essays in Criticism*, for which he wrote, as a provocative opening, 'The Function of Criticism at the Present Time'—his first formal statement of his critical position since the 1853 preface, and logically continuous from it. . . .

From Chapter 7 of *The Literary Critics*, Chatto and Windus, London, 1964, revised edition, pp. 131–6.

# The Critic: A Summing-up

It is unfortunate that Arnold's appreciation of the artistic potentialities of the novel should have remained relatively undeveloped. Admittedly, his poem 'Haworth Churchyard' contains one of the earliest tributes to the power of *Wuthering Heights*; he has essays on George Sand and Tolstoy, in the latter of which he contrasts the Russian's treatment of Anna Karenina with Flaubert's hounding down of Emma Bovary; he makes references in this and other essays to various English novelists; and it would seem from his note-books that during his last years novels were securing an increased, though still small, share of his reading-time. But this hardly amounts to a sustained, serious interest in his own age's main form of literary expression; and nowhere does he utter an opinion on the work of that novelist whom more than any other he was fitted sympathetically to understand, George Eliot.

In so far as he is a strictly literary critic, he is mainly a critic of poetry; and his rank must be determined by such things as his lectures *On Translating Homer* and his essays 'Heinrich Heine', 'Wordsworth', 'Byron' and 'The Study of Poetry'. Even here, however, his admiration for the grand style causes him, as I have already remarked, to undervalue colloquialism and complexity. Nor is this his only conspicuous limitation. Despite his admiration for French civilization, he is notably unappreciative of French poetry. Comparing France's 'established national metre for high poetry', the rhymed alexandrine, with English blank verse, he insists, in 'Maurice de Guérin' and again in 'The French Play in London', that it is, like the heroic couplet of eighteenth-century England, 'a form radically inadequate and inferior'.

Readers occasionally allege a more general disability, namely, that he tries to measure poetry by an arbitrary external standard. Those who dread some such dictatorial design will naturally find utterances upon which to feed their apprehensions. But to do so is to forget Arnold's steady insistence that criticism is essentially the exercise of curiosity and that the really valuable judgment forms itself almost insensibly in the course of an attempt 'to see the object as in itself it really is'.

What literary judgment is concerned with is the object's power of satisfying, in the words of the 1853 'Preface', 'the great primary human affections: . . . those elementary feelings which subsist permanently in the race, and which are independent of time'. When Arnold recommends the use of touchstone-quotations, he is simply suggesting that readers can, by reminding themselves of poetry which has moved them at this level in the past, help themselves to a more secure judgment of that which actually confronts them. . . .

Distinguished as is Arnold's achievement in the best of his criticism of particular works and particular authors, it is probably less important than his achievement as a spokesman for criticism itself, as a champion of literary culture. 'The Function of Criticism at the Present Time' is both the classical apologia for the role which Arnold himself sustained with such effect and the classical statement of the liberal principles which ideally should guide its performance. 'The Literary Influence of Academies' is a persuasive reminder of the authority of standards of criticism. A general disregard for these would produce consequences which would not be confined to literature; and there was much in Arnold's environment, as there is in ours, to discourage any regard for them. So in *Culture and Anarchy* Arnold turns his attention to this environment and produces the wisest and wittiest of his longer prose works. His lively comic sense, wide acquaintance with English life, quick perceptions, alert intelligence, and fundamental seriousness are all evident here. Compared with these works in which he draws so extensively on his powers and experience, Arnold's poetry appears narrow in theme and monotonous in tone and feeling. To say so much is not, of course, to deny its sincerity and charm; nor is it to forget its occasional extraordinary power.

In his various prose writings, it is above all Arnold's sanity, his clear sense of things as they are, which is impressive. None of the other Victorian prophets with whom he is sometimes bracketed can claim this quality in anything like the same degree. Beside him, Carlyle looks grotesquely prejudiced, Ruskin febrile and unbalanced, Morris irresponsibly escapist. Even Mill, despite the saintliness of his rationalism, looks like the victim of a system.

To Arnold, a system was merely a mechanism for falsifying one's perceptions. In Frederic Harrison's 'Culture: A Dialogue', Arminius blames Arnold for lacking a philosophy with 'coherent[,] . . . interdependent, subordinate, and derivative' principles. Arnold saw his opportunity; the accusation was a perfect target for his ridicule, and he kept it under steady and shattering fire. In 'A French Critic on Goethe', he describes systematic literary criticism, by which he means criticism which pronounces judgment not in accordance with what it finds in the text but in accordance with some external system of beliefs, as 'the most worthless of all'.

Without relying upon any such external system for support, Arnold speaks with a quiet confidence in the justness of his particular perceptions. As we have seen, he is hard to please; but even his dissatisfaction with a book or institution or dogma usually finds delicate and urbane expression. So much so that a contemporary rightly credited him with having helped appreciably 'to raise our standard of criticism above that of the old slashing, rough-and-ready clubmen of literature'.

At the same time, it must be admitted that he can seem distinctly supercilious. Hearing of his death, an acquaintance was moved to exclaim, 'Poor Arnold! he won't like God'. A lifelong friend gives an excellent description of the effect of his polite, aloof raillery in controversy. 'It cannot be denied that he had the art, when he chose to use it, of making those whom he criticised look supremely ridiculous, and people put into such a position do not always see the fun of it so clearly as others. Nay, they are apt sometimes to get very angry, and to curse and swear (in a literary sense) so as to lay themselves open to fresh castigation from their amused tormentor. All the more if the punishment is bestowed with imperturbable good humour, with serene superiority and with an air of innocence and wonder very funny but very exasperating.' So important was controversy in Arnold's literary life that no account of his criticism could be complete without the introduction of such opponents as F. W. Newman and Fitzjames Stephen.

Arnold's self-assurance did not impair his fair-mindedness. He strove to achieve a full view of things even in circumstances in which it might have seemed that a partial view would provide a more effective basis for prompt and vigorous action. I have already quoted examples of those returns upon himself which testify so clearly to his flexibility, his moderation, and his 'justness of spirit'; and these are qualities which may be felt throughout his work.

Sane, confident, urbane, and fair-minded; experienced and perceptive; free from any compulsion to crush his notions into a system—Arnold is indubitably the central man of letters of his age. Its most distinguished poet is the author of the words which I should like to set down in conclusion. Replying to a friend who evidently disliked Arnold's tone, G. M. Hopkins says: 'I do not like your calling Matthew Arnold Mr Kidglove Cocksure. I have more reason than you for disagreeing with him and thinking him very wrong, but nevertheless I am sure he is a rare genius and a great critic.'

From the last chapter of *Matthew Arnold*, Longmans, London, New York, Toronto, 1955, pp. 171–4.

# Select Bibliography

## THE WORKS OF MATTHEW ARNOLD

There are two important editions of Arnold's poetry. *The Poetical Works of Matthew Arnold*, edited by C. B. Tinker and H. F. Lowry, Oxford University Press, 1950, contains Arnold's explanatory notes, and footnotes record his alterations of the text for successive editions. Kenneth Allott's edition of *The Poems of Matthew Arnold* was published by Longmans in 1965, the first volume in their series of 'Annotated English Poets'. Allott's headnotes to individual poems are very useful.

The standard edition of the prose is *The Complete Prose Works of Matthew Arnold*, edited by R. H. Super for the University of Michigan Press, Ann Arbor. The first volume was published in 1960 and a number have now appeared including *Lectures and Essays in Criticism*, 1962, and *Culture and Anarchy*, 1965. For material not yet available in Dr Super's fine edition, students may consult the fifteen-volume *Works of Matthew Arnold*, published in 1903-4 by Macmillan, or *Essays, Letters and Reviews by Matthew Arnold*, edited by Fraser Neiman, for Harvard University Press, 1960. An excellent one-volume selection of the prose, edited by P. J. Keating for Penguin Books, was published in 1970.

The breadth of Arnold's reading in six languages is reflected in *The Notebooks of Matthew Arnold*, edited by H. F. Lowry, Karl Young and W. H. Dunn, Oxford University Press, 1952.

## BIOGRAPHY AND LETTERS

It was Arnold's wish that his biography should not be written. There is as yet no collected edition of his letters; A. K. Davis, however, has produced *Matthew Arnold's Letters, a Descriptive Checklist*, published by the University Press of Virginia, Charlottesville, 1968, which lists 2,658 letters, more than half of them so far unpublished. The most important volume of letters published is *The Letters of Matthew Arnold to Arthur Hugh Clough*, Oxford University Press, 1932, splendidly edited by H. F. Lowry. Two other collections are *The Letters of Matthew Arnold 1848-1888*, edited in two volumes by G. W. E. Russell, Macmillan, London, 1895, and *Unpublished Letters of Matthew Arnold*, edited by Arnold Whitridge, Yale University Press, 1923.

## BIBLIOGRAPHY

Volume 15 of Macmillan's *Works of Matthew Arnold* includes T. B. Smart's *Bibliography of Matthew Arnold*, but this contains no item published after 1891.

The most useful account of criticism is to be found in *The Victorian Poets: a Guide to Research*, edited by F. E. Faverty, the second edition of which was published by Harvard University Press in 1968. *Victorian*

*Poetry*, the quarterly journal published by West Virginia University, contains a useful annual survey of significant work of the previous year. The Oxford University Press volume, *English Poetry: Select Bibliographical Guides*, 1971, edited by A. E. Dyson has a comprehensive chapter on Arnold by James Bertram.

## CRITICAL STUDIES:

(*a*) BOOKS:

Among the many studies of different aspects of Matthew Arnold's work the best are:

C. B. Tinker and H. F. Lowry, *The Poetry of Matthew Arnold: a Commentary*, Oxford University Press, 1940. (This is not a work of interpretative criticism but a collection of background information of the kind that Allott incorporates into his edition.)

Lionel Trilling, *Matthew Arnold*, Columbia University Press, New York and George Allen and Unwin, London, 2nd edition, 1949; (the most important study of Arnold's thought).

W. F. Connell, *The Educational Thought and Influence of Matthew Arnold*. Routledge & Kegan Paul, London, 1950.

D. G. James, *Matthew Arnold and the Decline of English Romanticism*, Oxford University Press, 1961.

A. Dwight Culler, *Imaginative Reason: the Poetry of Matthew Arnold*, Yale University Press, New Haven, Conn. and London, 1966; (an excellent criticism of the poetry).

G. Robert Stange, *Matthew Arnold: the Poet as Humanist*, Princeton University Press, 1967.

A. Roper, *Arnold's Poetic Landscapes*, Johns Hopkins Press, Baltimore, 1969; (a sensitive study somewhat handicapped by its thesis).

(*b*) ARTICLES AND CHAPTERS IN GENERAL WORKS (*excluding* those selected for this volume):

K. Allott, 'A Background for "Empedocles on Etna" ', *Essays and Studies*, John Murray, London, 1968, pp. 80–100.

Vincent Buckley, *Poetry and Morality*, Chatto and Windus, London, 1959; (an advanced account of Arnold, Eliot and Leavis as critics).

S. M. B. Coulling, 'Matthew Arnold's 1853 Preface: its Origin and Aftermath', *Victorian Studies*, Vol. 7, 1964, pp. 233–63.

J. P. Curgenven, 'The Scholar-Gipsy: a Study of the Growth, Meaning, and Integration of a Poem', *Litera*, Vol. 2, 1955, pp. 41–58; Vol. 3, 1956, pp. 1–13. (This Turkish periodical is virtually unobtainable but the article may be republished elsewhere.)

D. J. DeLaura, 'Arnold and Carlyle', *PMLA*, Vol. 79, 1964, pp. 104–29.

T. S. Eliot, *The Use of Poetry and the Use of Criticism*, Faber and Faber, London, 1933, pp. 103–19.

E. D. H. Johnson, *The Alien Vision of Victorian Poetry*, Princeton University Press, 1952.

G. Wilson Knight, 'The Scholar-Gipsy: an Interpretation', *Review of English Studies*, N.S., Vol. 6, 1955, pp. 53–62.

F. R. Leavis, *The Common Pursuit*, Penguin Books, Harmondsworth, 1962, pp. 29–32. *Education and the University*, 2nd ed., Chatto and Windus, London, 1948, pp. 73–6.

K. Tillotson, ' "Yes: in the Sea of Life" ', *Review of English Studies*, N.S., Vol. 3, 1952, pp. 346–64. Reprinted in *Mid-Victorian Studies*, The Athlone Press, London, 1963, pp. 157–79.